Poems
from
an Emerald Asteroid

Also by Colin MacCallum

Mainly Sentimental - 250 Poems of a Lifetime

Sea, Sky and Dreams
(An anthology of poetry from Hornby and Denman Islands)

The Bang Family on Strømsø
(A family history by Cathinco Bang,
translated by Colin from the Norwegian)

✳❤✳

Poems

from

an Emerald Asteroid

by

Colin MacCallum, PEng

If you've never read poetry before,
This book holds much pleasure in store,
With words that all rhyme
And lines that beat time:
Poems of life, loving, laughter - and more!

✳❤✳

※❤※

First published 2004
First impression: 1000 softcover; 200 hardcover

Published by
MacCallum Boiler Associates Inc.
~~4996 Bella Vista Crescent~~
~~Nanaimo, BC~~
~~V9V 1M5~~
~~Canada~~   shaw.ca
                     e-mail: maccallu@~~mars.ark.com~~

Published with no financial assistance from the taxpayer.

Photographs by Jim MacCallum, West Vancouver, and Bob Cain, Hornby Island, as indicated. Other photos are credited as shown, or are family photos.

Cover layout concept by Colin MacCallum; aerial photo by Sasha LeBaron; cover design by Murray Oates.

Printed and bound in Canada by Friesens Corporation.

Canadian Cataloguing in Publication Data

MacCallum, C., 1935-

   Poems from an Emerald Asteroid / C. MacCallum

   ISBN 1-55383-023-7

   1. Canadian poetry (English) - 21st century.

Now on Amazon

※❤※

✳❤✳

INTRODUCTION

Now living in Nanaimo, Colin was an integral part of Hornby Island life for ten years. He is an engineer by profession, a fiercely competitive golfer and tennis/badminton player and above all, a social animal in the finest sense of the expression.

He was the ideal person for wine steward in the local wine club. On one occasion, discussing new memberships to our club, we felt it essential to avoid people who may drink in excess. Colin observed "Such people are probably already members" and had by this time ensured that most of us already drank to excess, by his liberality in serving the wine!

With his Scottish background and love of poetry and song, Colin was the first choice to lead Robert Burns celebrations in our community. I can always remember Colin with the help of another Scot, leading the most vigorous sing-along ever held at the community hall. And then there was the New Year's party complete with Auld Lang Syne and champagne. Most memorable was Colin's toast "To Absent Friends". How appropriate a thought, for the ending of one year and the beginning of another.

Colin has many facets to his personality, therefore it is not surprising that he has produced this kaleidoscope of poetry - warm and moving, sometimes sentimental and romantic, sometimes reminiscent of times gone by. Many poems are reminders of pleasant things. Some are philosophical musings about the human condition. Topics are often treated with humour, occasionally ironic, but more often in fun. Something for everyone.

Doug Carrick
Hornby Island

❋❤❋

Colin MacCallum in 2004

FOREWORD

These poems are a sequel to my earlier book, "Mainly Sentimental" which presented 250 poems of my lifetime up to the age of sixty, in 1995. All of them are new, except for a couple which were written earlier and have had a verse or two added.

The poems are really windows into the mind of a person approaching 70 - surely, one day, your mind. Unlike fiction, they reveal thoughts that most of us don't normally talk about. In them, I shuffle, run, dance or leap - I revel in an unusual word in a limerick, I rejoice in a happy moment, or ache with longing and nostalgia for Scotland, for Gothenburg, for "vanished Youth, Innocence, and friends".

Acknowledgements

My many thanks for ongoing encouragement are due to my wife, Jane and to the rest of my family and friends who have been supportive over the years. The First Edition on Hornby Island has published my poems from time to time and I have particularly appreciated the unsolicited and positive comments on these poems in chance encounters with friends and acquaintances in the Co-op and elsewhere.

I also must acknowledge the contribution of my intermittent insomnia which has afforded me time to write such stuff!

Most of the photographs, those of Hornby Island in particular, were provided by Bob Cain. On page 18, the photos of Sarah, my grand-niece, are by Photography by Richard in Santa Maria, CA and by Susan Goldman who wrote an interesting piece in the Santa Maria Times. My brother Jim in West Vancouver, took several of the other photographs and copied and rejuvenated a number of older family photos. Murray Oates, my step-son, designed the softcover with its delightful colours.

Colin MacCallum
Nanaimo, BC
September 2004

 iii

✳❤✳

Some Comments from the Critics

"..... kaleidoscope of poetry - warm and moving, sometimes sentimental and romantic, sometimes reminiscent of times gone by. .... treated with humour, occasionally ironic, but more often in fun. Something for everyone."
Doug Carrick, Hornby Island

"Colin writes verse in his own way for his own reasons and doesn't let prevailing literary fashion stand in his way. For that I admire him."
Howard White, Harbour Publishing, Madeira Park, BC

"Poems from an Emerald Asteroid is filled with humour and *joie de vivre*. In his own, unique way, Colin touches on all aspects of life. He calls up pictures which we all can identify with, some serious, some beautiful and some will make us chuckle. If you like poetry that rhymes, this is the book you'll enjoy."
Jos Kollee, Writer, Editor/Publisher IRIS magazine

"While reading Colin's poems, images were springing into my mind. It seemed an uncanny visual experience. I had no trouble choosing photographs to match his poetry. Although it feels like collaboration, there was none, unless you count a similarity of experience and vision. If my photographs were turned into poetry, these poems come as close to their essence as could be imagined."
Bob Cain, Photographer, Hornby Island

✳♥✳

"I sell all sorts of books, including poetry, but normally I wouldn't, myself, read poetry - I'm not a poetry guy - but these poems are really readable - and very entertaining!"
John Falconer, Falconer Books,
Nanaimo, BC

"In this book of delightful rhymes and lyrics, MacCallum becomes the good-humoured, energetic Scot I have known personally and also as editor of the book of poems, "Sea, Sky and Dreams", a composite of Hornby and Denman Island poets and their offerings.

"Poems from an Emerald Asteroid" brings us a wide spectrum of events and opinions in the author's life, much of it in the tradition of Robbie Burns wherein he gives us the most literal of the Scottish brogue in verse.

For me, the richness of "Emerald Asteroid"; once opened, was difficult to leave, and this is a credit to any author, more so to this Jolly Scot, who truly writes from the hip, like it or not!"
Bill Yeomans, Hornby Island

"Colin's poetry is rhythmically, rhymingly and colourfully reflective of his life, both on Hornby and elsewhere. I especially enjoyed the witty limericks and, inspired, tried to fashion my review of his new volume as a limerick as well - only to give up - they are incredibly difficult to write! A really fun book!"
Carol Martin Quin, Old Rose Garden,
Hornby Island

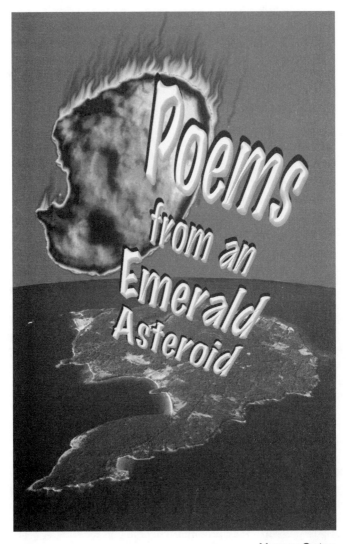

Murray Oates

Comet Wild 2 about 20,000 ft above Hornby Island
- and closing

❤

To Jane

Believe me, if all those endearing young charms,
Which I gaze on so fondly today,
Were to fade by tomorrow, and fleet in my arms,
Like fairy gifts fading away,
Thou would'st still be adored, as this moment thou art,
Let thy lovliness fade as it will,
And around the dear ruin each wish of my heart
Would entwine itself verdantly still.

Thomas Moore (1779-1852)

✳❤✳

CONTENTS

✱❤✱

✳♥✳

PUSSYCAT POEMS

Pussycat, Pussycat, You're Eighteen!

Sophie, our pussycat, 's just turned eighteen,
A poem seems especially apt -
Not many pussycats live to this age -
Just think of the milk that she's lapped!

And think of the cat-food she's eaten, to date,
With barely a morsel of waste!
Then there's the sparrows
　　　　　　　　she's scared into flight,
And all of the mice that she's chased!

There's many a Tom-cat she's scratched on the nose
And, hissing, has shown him his place,
Of course there were others she's welcomed around
- They left with a smile on their face!

Once, at eleven, she got lost in the bush,
Pender Island - the scene of her trip -
Five months of privation before she turned up -
Thin - with a hop and a skip!

Although she's so ancient, her paws are still white,
Dark coat - a bit thin here and there -
Her back's a bit bony - she's lost all her fat -
She's deaf, but I know she's a happy old cat
As she purrs on the arm of my chair!

✳♥✳　o　✳♥✳

✻❤✻

Poor Old Sophie

She never made it through the operation on her paw,
Her heart kept beating, but her breathing stopped.
We'd been most reluctant to submit her to the saw,
But, with cancer now, there isn't much to opt.

I brought her home, so quiet and still, not a movement there
And thought of all the pleasure we'd derived
Through eighteen years of knowing her,
                              the things that she'd survived,
And buried her, beneath her tree, beside her wooden chair.

She'll never come to meet us now,
                              she'll never come to greet us now,
Her tail erect, with pleasure, from her hide;
She'd hear the car and hurry down, while purring, like a bride,
As quickly as her dignity 'd allow.

We see her basket, empty now, expect her all around;
At breakfast time she'd beg for Marmite, lick your finger clean;
Sit beside you, on your lap, and then, there was the sound
She'd make for my attention,
                              at the door she'd shake the screen.

It's bad enough to know we'll never see our cat again,
But, worse, I hear her crying in the darkness and the rain.

✳❤✳

Emily

We have a little kitten now, the sweetest little thing,
She hops and skips and capers,
                          playing with paper or with string;
Soft and dainty little paws, a tiny, button nose,
She makes you feel quite sleepy, lying, lolling in repose.

She nibbles at my finger and she whispers in my ear,
Coquettish, like a little girl, with eyes so blue and clear.
She snoozes on the sofa and she curls up in a hat,
She's a pretty little kitten and she'll be a lovely cat!

✳❤✳

Glasgow - Changed, But Unchanged

To trace my steps from school to home,
To see the paths we used to roam,
To show my son where I have been,
To tell of things that I have seen,
    Is more than simple pleasure.

Kelvin's banks are greener now,
The soot has gone from leaf and bough,
The buildings, all are red or gold
Instead of black, in days of old
    And folk have much more leisure.

The trams have gone, the cobbles too,
The lowering skies transformed to blue,
The river's smell is not the same
And quenched is Dixon's Blazes' flame;
    There's change on every side.

Now, cars are parked on every street
That knew the sound of childhood feet;
Doors on closes bar the way
To greens and dykes where we would play
    And run and jump and hide.

Other curtains proudly grace
What once was Auntie Nancy's place
And flowers now bloom, where mud and grass
Concealed the bricks and broken glass
    - You feel the city's pride!

But lovers still go arm in arm,
The kids retain their friendly charm,
Cheery folk still catch your eye
And nod a greeting, passing by
    - And I'm the same, inside.

✳❤✳

Cousins Jean Mitchell and Jim MacCallum, in Greenlaw, 1939

Jean died in Fish Hoek, Republic of South Africa, on 3rd April 2003.

✳❤✳

Once Upon A Time

Remember crawling through the leaves,
Their touch, their sound, their smell?
Remember racing round the park
And "chases" by the well?
Kick-the-can and hide-and-seek,
Cops and robbers too;
It seems like yesterday to me
And much the same to you!

Chorus: How can it be that Yesterday
- so bright, so clear - so far, so near -
Can suddenly be "Once upon a time"?

We climbed the hills to see the view,
We tumbled through the greens,
We raced along the tops of walls,
And squabbled with our frien's.
We picnicked with the Sunday School,
Tramcarred to the Zoo.
I haven't changed a bit inside
- But neither then, have you!

We wandered down by Kelvin's banks
With hawthorn trees in bloom;
We snuggled 'neath a cosy rug
In the firelight's flick'ring gloom;
Felt the thrilling happiness -
Young love, fond and true
And stored a million memories
For me and, sweet, for you.

How can it be that Yesterday
- so bright, so clear - so far, so near -
Can suddenly be "Once upon a time"?

The High School of Glasgow - in 1950

To start the day each morning
The janny rang the bell;
You heard its tolling down the street
And had to run like hell!

You'd hear its urgent summons
And know that you were late
And Retribution waited
As you skittered through the gate!

At 10, we pushed our Dinky Toys -
The farthest won the game.
Class photographs - I have them yet
And still recall each name.

I seldom did my homework
And fell behind a lot;
The motivation wasn't there
- And who would be a swot!

It was no bed of roses -
The teachers used "The Strap",
But one thing very certain was
You learned to shut your trap!

We had our share of bullies
I still recall the fear
Of torture in the lavatories
- A red and twisted ear.

If you were small and cheeky
Then danger lurked for you
And if you weren't fleet of foot
Then you'd be black and blue!

I'd love to list those bullies
And hurt them, line by line,
But I'd hate to hurt their feelings
- Tho' those buggers sure hurt mine!

✳❤✳

Our rugby team went down to Kiel
I was twelve - and small.
A fixture screw-up saw them field
Giants - ten feet tall!

They beat us sixty-three to nil
In mud and pouring rain.
I was crushed as full-back
And I never played again!

Each steamy bath at Anniesland
Could hold three rugby teams;
The water soon was turgid, black
Beyond your wildest dreams!

I ran the line for sev'ral years
And wrote up all the games
I saw - and heard - two broken legs
But don't recall the names.

Forms Three and Four were really bad
My marks went down the drain
I remember my report cards
Were a constant source of pain!

Form Five was best - I did it twice
And maths became a breeze
Thanks to one MacDonald
Who taught with practised ease.

My final year was lots of fun -
I even learned to dance -
McEwan's (Roger) was the place
A hotbed of romance!

Schoolboy life was simpler then -
None of us had cars -
But for my time at Glasgow High
I thank my lucky stars!

Dowanhill Church Transformation

Sunday School benches have now been replaced
By the stools of a popular bar!
Where once the lassies were proper and chaste
There's leather and lipstick, powder and paint!
Gone are the pictures of hero and saint
And the princes who followed a star.

I wonder what old Dr Baxter would think
- Bright eyes under steep, craggy brow -
I think that, like me, he'd be needing a drink
At the sight of the theatre, the lighting, the stage,
The band-members strutting in clothes all the rage
- Things the Kirk wouldn't allow!

✳❤✳

St ABBS AND SCOTLAND

Storm-bound in St Abbs

See the waves' majestic splendour
Crash on the craggy, rock-bound shore,
Creaming crest and foaming whiteness,
Troughs expose the rocks once more.

Seabirds whirl and stall and plummet,
Sense each joyous, upward blast,
Flock to play in gay abandon,
Race the spindrift, skyward cast.

Breakers bar the harbour entrance
Hurled by the eastern, raging gale
That whistles in the whipping rigging,
Tears away the seagulls' wail.

Fish-boats huddle in the shelter,
Safe by the inner harbour wall;
I stand, transfixed by the foaming welter,
Caught in the storm-tossed breakers' thrall.

The Voices of the Sea

There's a spot on the foreshore at Coldingham Sands
That catches the voice of the sea,
That amplifies even the tiniest sound
And returns it, so clearly, to me.

When darkling storm-clouds westward race
The waves that crash and shatter there,
A tortured maelstrom, spuming white
As ancient mermaid's tangled hair,
A deeply thundering rumble fills
The sky, my ears, my soul, my all;
A mighty engine strains to leave
Poseidon's main departure hall.

But when the evening 's mild and still
And tiny wavelets lap the shore,
The voices whisper, down the years,
As once they murmured, long before.
They tell of picnics on the sands,
Of orange cake, with icing, cream,
Of childhood chums, of uncles, aunts,
Clear, in a fond-remembered dream;
Friends and lovers, hand in hand,
In gloaming, warm, or moonlight gleam,
Of breathless whispers, promised love,
Sweet moments that we can't redeem.

St Abbs Head Nunnery - Remains of

Up by The Head where the seagulls shriek
And the red rocks crumble away,
There's a pile of stones that I wish could speak -
I wonder, what would they say?

They'd tell the tale of the girls that came,
With beliefs of hope and love
Love for their Lord and the sweet Christ's name
And praise for the stars above.

Tales of the primitive life they led
In their cassocks, grey or brown,
With straw or with bulrushes for their bed
And miles to the nearest town.

It might be years 'til they'd see their kin,
Their loved ones, fond and dear,
While a mother's laugh or a brother's grin
Remained but a memory, clear.

Scant meals on a bench in a draughty hall,
Twenty-five by seventy feet long,
With the prayers and the bells and religion's thrall
And their voices raised in song.

On a soaring crag o'er a roaring wave,
With a drop to terrify some,
They'd work and pray, and they'd scrape and save
With their hopes of Kingdom Come.

Their times were light in the summer time,
Though their days were long and hard,
But bleak were the rooms, all frosty rime,
With winter's icy shard.

When the rain was ice and the snow was driven
Through the window slits and doors,
Then their fears of Hell and their hopes of Heaven
Would help them through their chores.

There'd be likes and dislikes, friendships too,
'Tween the nuns both young and old,
There'd be sly, and spry, and eyes of blue,
And girls both shy and bold.

And once or twice, came a horrid spring
When fear was on every lip
And the distant flash of a seagull's wing
Was a fearsome Viking ship.

All the nuns would pray in the good Lord's name
And burn a holy candle,
But the Vikings came with their sword and flame,
Like the Jute, and Goth, and Vandal.

Some nuns met death by their own cell door
And some were carried away,
Mistress-to-be of a Viking floor
Where a Viking's children play.

I sit on the stones, but the stones can't talk,
Though they whisper in back of my knees
I shiver, I stand and go on with my walk
And their memories blow in the breeze.

✳❤✳

Look Out - I'm Coming!!!

Chorus:
    I sauntered over Rannoch and I munched upon my bannock
    And bathed in crystal pools beneath the sky;
    And I bounded through the heather
    Wi' never time tae blether,
    Cape Wrath! I'm comin' - laugh-ter in my eye!

I left George Square and waved her
                 and I wished I could have saved her
The sadness of farewell that made her cry;
I left her there behind me, fair,
My tears did hotly blind me there
But they couldnae damp the laughter in my eye!

If I said I took Glen Falloch on the other side of Balloch,
Then sure as shootin', I'd be kidding you!
But the Balloch lassies smiled tae me,
Wi' lips sae red, beguiling me,
And the sunbeams they were brightly smiling too!

I camped there by sweet Lomond,
                 oh sae ghostly in the gloamin',
I missed Patricia - wished her there wi' me!
I pitched my little tentie noo
And ate my fill and plenty too
And a million midges kept me companee!

Tae climb tae Crianlarich, ye will need yer bowl o' parritch,
I freewheeled then tae bonny wee Tyndrum;
I thought o' hearth an' o' my hame
But I was seekin' fortune, fame -
I'm better here than sittin' on my bum!

At Bridge of Orchy turn-off, a' the mist began tae burn off,
My breakfast but a mem'ry, hours ago!
Had dinner wi' a signalman,
                    six dochters they were single, man!
An' I left them there wi' weary feet an' slow!

Loch Treig upon the morrow - Loch Treig's the loch o' sorrow -
That day it glittered brightly, powder blue.
The country here is really wild - it's no' a place for ony child,
Commandos trained here back in 'forty-two.

By Ness I got a blister and I wished my little sister
Was there tae put a plaster on my heel.
But though I was a-limping, the miles were surely crimping,
As I walked I sang of herring in my creel!

A lass I met in Beauly, I could sure have loved her, truly,
Perhaps she could have been the girl for me.
I kissed her by the river there, but I could never marry her,
For she was one of merry triplets three!

Up through Tain and Dingwall, there I had nae time for kingball,
Dodgieball or kick-the-can wi' you.
And by Loch Shin in Sutherland,
                    I cursed the Duke who owned the land
And wished I owned a tiny bittie too!

The tenth day came a-dawning -
                    it was misty, cool that morning;
My step was light, my heel was free from pain!
I sang with all my main and might
                    tae see that simply glorious sight -
Cape Wrath in ab-sol-utely pissing rain!

✳❤✳

Spring in the Scottish Borders

How green and how lovely the meadows in March,
The primroses under the trees,
The buds all a-greening on willow and larch,
While the daffodils dance in the breeze.

White blossom, scattered at random it seems,
In gardens and hedgerows around,
Forsythia beckons with rich golden streams
And the doves with their cooing abound.

Lambs full of joyful fun
Skip with a stumbling run
Or soak up the sleepy sun.

See how our fingers cling,
Hear how our spirits sing,
To greet yet another spring.

✳❤✳

REMINISCENCES

✳❤✳

Salad Days in Gothenburg at Midsummer

    I see the students celebrate
    The days in which they graduate -
        Young men laughing,
        Young girls whooping,
    Dresses, white, both short and long,
    Young eyes filled with springtime's song.

    Older folks at sidewalk tables,
    On the street to see the show,
        Smiling inward,
        Smiling outward,
    Knowing things the kids don't know -
    But where did all our summers go?

♥

On First Hearing Charlotte Church

I heard an angel singing,
Her eyes a sleepy blue,
With innocence and love of life
And laughter shining through.

I heard an angel singing
In tones so true and sweet
That princes, popes and potentates
All worship at her feet.

I heard an angel singing,
A girl of just thirteen,
Her voice as pure as platinum
With luminescent sheen
And silver echoes lingering,
A rosebud of a queen.

Sarah - 8 Years Old

Dancing, singing, phone-bell ringing;
Chatter, patter, pigtails swinging.
Confident and captivating,
Gaze, direct and worldly-wise,
Yet underneath she's meditating,
    Regretful of her tiny size.
With sunbeams from the ripples shining,
    Shining from her eyes.

Sarah   Susan Goldman

Metamorphosis

Sarah at her graduation
Radiates sophistication,
Drives her truck with verve and glee,
Just half the height of you and me!
What a transformation!

Sarah   Richard Photo

✳❤✳

New Moon Magic

Startling, bright, in the western sky,
A delicate crescent of August moon
Like a longship's sail in the setting sun.
(Hear the seabirds' haunting cry!)

Like a golden torque on a maiden's arm
In an ancient campfire's glow,
Or a shining crown on a princely brow
In a palace, long ago;
Like the lamp-lit curve of a rounded breast,
To a wanton lover's eye.

Minutes of beauty, then gone like a dream,
All passion spent,
Like love, requited,
Leaving Earth, beneath, benighted.

Tønsberg, Norway

Higgledy-piggledy houses
With colours so bright and so clean;
Mostly bright, dazzling white, or a rich, rusty red,
Yellow gold, misty blue, in between.

Ghostly, each Viking carouses
With whalers long home from the sea,
By the graves of the kings looking down on the town
Where the kids roller-blade on the quay.

✳❤✳

The Auld Smithy

The jingle of the harness,
A huge horse shakes his head,
The evening shadows deepen by the door,
The showering sparks spring brightly,
Starry-white, then red,
Then swiftly blacken, dying, on the floor.
"Stand back now, laddie." grunts the smith
As I edge ever nearer
To see the wonders of the forge,
Its secrets ever clearer,
His voice so quiet, commanding,
The horse pricks up his ears,
A tone of voice that brooks no interferer.

Inside, the glowing fireplace,
The anvil's ringing sound,
The ready hammers, horseshoes, in their place
And scythe-blades glitter whitely
In darkness quite profound;
I feel the radiation on my face.
Behind me, softly falling snow
In wetness quickly thawing,
While in the treetops' tracery
The crows' insistent cawing
And also, quietly standing,
A mother with her child,
Approaching, looking, smiling, then withdrawing.

❤

The ancient smithy bustles
Much more than former times
And people come and go the whole day through;
While every waitress hustles,
A wall-clock quietly chimes
And lunch is served from midday on, 'til two.
I sit and sip my coffee there,
The cup is hot and brimming.
The snow still falls, the trees are bare,
But all my thoughts are swimming -
I see majestic horses,
The forge's ruddy glare
Reflected in the door-knob's brassy trimming.

Ashley and Christopher

❤

A Fairy Child

This little girl is daisy-sweet
With dainty little hands and feet
One moment still, one moment fleet,
        Now there, now here.

Her skin is blemish-free and clear,
She runs, as graceful as a deer
Startled by some sudden fear,
        A woodland sprite.

Her eyes are palest blue and bright
Like stars that twinkle in the night
And yet they have a pensive light
        From time to time.

And on my shoulder she would climb
And laugh in joyous pantomime,
A rippling giggle, quite sublime,
        Enraptured in a race.

Thick fair hair around her face,
I see her leaning, full of grace
And gazing into empty space.
        At what - who knows?

Fairest cheeks, a tiny nose,
The sweetest mouth in palest rose,
So animate, yet, in repose
        So calm, serene.

A dainty swimsuit, blue and green,
Golden limbs, all flashing, clean,
She could be a faerie queen,
        This lovely little girl.

✳❤✳

The Lucia Tradition

Every year, in Sweden, on the 13th of December, all the Daddies are up early. They waken the children quietly. Together, they prepare a pretty tray with coffee and ginger cookies. Then, the children and Daddy, in a candlelight procession, singing the Saint Lucia song, enter their parents' bedroom and "waken" Mummy.

It is difficult not to be moved by the sight of the little children, pajama-clad, or dressed in long, white gowns, singing sweetly, with their candlelight sparkling in their eyes. The same ceremony is repeated in most offices, factories and restaurants throughout the day, with a young girl as Saint Lucia with a crown of candles, followed by a train of other girls, and star-boys, all bearing candles and singing the Lucia song written by Arvid Rosén and which I have translated here.

> Nightly, go heavy hearts
> Round farm and steading;
> On earth, where Sun departs,
> Shadows are spreading.
> Then on our darkest night,
> Comes with her shining light,
> Sankta Lucia! Sankta Lucia!
>
> Night-darkling, huge and still.
> Hark, something's stirring!
> In all our silent rooms,
> Wingbeats are whisp'ring!
> Stands on our threshold there,
> White-clad, lights in her hair,
> Sankta Lucia! Sankta Lucia!
>
> "Darkness shall fly away
> Through earthly portals!"
> She brings such wonderful
> Words to us mortals!
> "Daylight, again renewed,
> Will rise, all rosy-hued!"
> Sankta Lucia! Sankta Lucia!

Sleeping Draught

Upon the map my finger traces,
In memory, I see the places,
Hear the voices, see the faces,
Some from long ago.

And in my mind the embers glow,
The thought ignites, the flickers grow;
I see the folks I used to know,
The roads we used to roam.

They say all highways lead to Rome
But I explore each house, each home,
Relaxing, just before I sleep.
Warm thoughts, like summer breezes, sweep
The ashes from my heart.

✳❤✳

The Generation Gap

One 1940s evening, I was thirteen (going on ten!)
We were looking at some photographs (we did that now and then)
Just four of us, myself of course, my brothers and a friend,
A group beneath the lamp, alive with patter!
While Mother sat there by the fire, with socks she had to mend,
Quietly listening to our chortles and our chatter.

We laughed at all the dresses, we jeered at all the hats,
Roared at "flappers", yowling like a load of Cheshire cats;
We mocked the men in "boaters", with their neatly-buttoned spats
And criticized each scene we were espying.
Our laughter reached crescendo at the swimsuit styles and that's
When I became aware that Mum was crying!

Horrified and silenced, we asked her what was wrong?
She dashed a tear, protesting that the maidens in each throng
Were sweet and lovely, elegant, in dresses short and long,
Compared to all our trashy, modern trends.
Had we but understood, she sang us Life's eternal song
Of vanished Youth, and Innocence, and friends.

✳❤✳

ABSENT FRIENDS

✳❤✳

Who Knows?

To "Absent Friends" we raise our glass
And toast them most sincerely
Ans as the years and decades pass
We miss them more severely.

We see those ranks of absent friends
Unfortunately swelling,
But when OUR earthly sojourn ends,
It's lucky, no one 's telling!

Hal   R.Cain

Hal Arnold

Indifferent to their ministrations,
Hal the centre of attention
On the beach; the First Responders;
Urgent work with good intention.

Other summer eves as lovely,
Down his private forest trail
To the beach, the evening ritual,
Swim - relate his latest tale.

Hal would chat and Hal would chuckle,
Widening grin and impish eye,
Full of anecdote and whimsy -
How we loved his humour - wry.

We'll see his shambling gait in mem'ry,
Or a younger Hal, and trim,
One moment grave, then sudden laughter,
A painting to remember him.

Hal the artist, Hal the rebel,
Hal the pilot, flac-torn sky,
Humourist and island cynic
With that twinkle in his eye.
Goodbye.

To Peter Izat

The photo shows our mothers in a class with many others,
Little girls with tunic dresses, happy smiles and flowing tresses,
In kindergarten, ninety years ago.

We met much later, you and I, the T.A., 5th/6th H.L.I.*,
Tartan trews on drill and mess nights, jaunty bonnets, fitted blues
And Jocks wi' drink, aggressively aglow.

I aye admired your upright grace,
your tennis shots had power and pace,
In squash, your strong, unerring aim,
and love of life, a blazing flame
As lively as a tumbling, mountain stream.

Splendid Scottish soldier, whom I'll miss until I die,
I see you in your bonny girls, your twinkling, clear-blue eye
And mannerisms, subtle as a dream.

* Territorial Army, 5th/6th Battalion Highland Light Infantry, Glasgow, Scotland

✳❤✳

My Friend

How can someone lie dying
On a gorgeous day like today,
When the sky is blue and the sea is bright
And the sea lions dip and play?

How can someone lie dying
When the sunbeams slant through the trees,
When the air is clear and the grass is green
And the crocuses beg to the bees?

There are sounds of distant crying
As a precious lifetime ends
And the pain 's still there and the parting hurts,
From so many, dearest friends.

I suppose when someone lies dying
On a gorgeous day like today,
That the world just shrinks to a tiny space
And the words that loved-ones say.

Peter MacKechnie Izat died on 21 February 2001, just a week before
his 62nd birthday, which would have been on 1 March. He fought his
cancer, day by day, for more than two years, until the very end.

✳❤✳

Steve Pope, PEng

Steve Pope, Professional Engineer,
Fiercely honest, slim, severe,
Dark-blue suit and polished shoe,
That quizzical eye as he looked at you,
Declaiming his view of Original Sin,
Turbine nozzles, the Money Supply,
As he rummaged for tobacco in his battered old tin.
He'd make his ammunition,
            weighing powder by the grain,
Cast his leaden bullets,
Or go hiking with his fam'ly in the rain.

No dope. A daredevil downhill skier,
Turbine expert, blade and gear.
Manner mild and gentle voice
The trails and the backwoods were ever his choice.
Hard to convince - and hard to direct,
Hard to rein in - and hard to deflect,
He would worry at a problem like a puppy with a bone
And arrive at a solution, quite peculiarly his own.

I would I could have seen him
                on the night before he died
Recite "The Ancient Mariner" beneath a starry sky.

For Big Jim McSherry - Friend of my Youth:

Comfort

Cold and white, the winter moon
Paints bitter shadows across the lawn;
So still the night, with silent tears
And many an hour to grieve 'til dawn.

I see him, tall and bright with Youth,
Boisterous, brash, and brave and bold,
His sudden chuckle, ready laugh
And think of how the good times rolled!

✳❤✳

On the death of Princess Margaret Rose:

Perhaps a Tiny Consolation
(to a Grieving Mother and Family)

How sad to see the grieving eye,
The trembling lip behind the veil
That separates your world and ours.
Yet we remember happy hours,
The princess from a fairy tale.
Our common grief we can't deny.

Now, captured in a picture frame
And safe in memory's casket, too,
Are moments from those happy times.
The tolling bells were wedding chimes.
We share those joyous hours with you,
For, underneath, we're all the same.

Remember now, through all the pain,
What we have lost is Heaven's gain.

Worlds Apart

So Ginsberg's dead! He was a bard
Who wielded words like lightning shards,
Was misconstrued by such as those
    Who lacked the wit
    To study it!

And Ginsberg said just what he meant
He'd never talk of "excrement"!
And he would seldom sniff the rose
    But stir the shit
    That nurtures it!

Alas! His flag was grabbed by others,
Twisted sisters, stunted brothers,
Spewing filth in crippled prose,
    Of craps in cans
    And nothing scans.

No discipline of rhyme or time,
Glorifying petty crime,
Unpleasant thoughts stuck up your nose,
    All Man's disgrace
    Shoved in your face.

But speech is free - thank God for that
And those who will, will read such scat,
    "Poems" that truly decompose;
    Sub-standard wares!
    I spit - who cares?

✳❤✳

LOVE AND ROMANCE

✳❤✳

Comfort and Joy

My arms were made to comfort you,
To hold you as we sway
To rhythms, timeless as the dawn;
My lips, to kiss your tears away.

My arms were made to hold you closely,
Warmly, tightly, night or day;
My lips were made to brush your cheek,
To frame the words that lovers say.

Come Dream with Me

Close your eyes and come a-strolling
Down a sunny, summer lane,
Where all the world is filled with magic
And you and I are young again.

Our world is all anticipation,
That longed-for smile, that shining face
And aching, burning, sweet temptation
Nestled in each warm embrace.

My Valentine - 2002

If I had one last poem to write
Before my final curtain falls
And as that final trumpet calls,
I'm sure I know what I would write.
I'd not waste words on diamonds, bright,
On Scotia's mountains, or Nepal's,
On Iguazu's majestic falls.
I'd write, instead, of my delight.

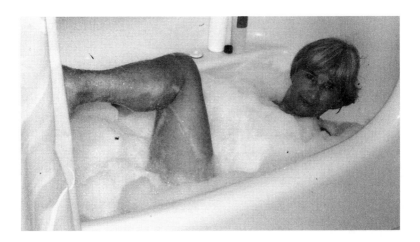

Jane, 1991

Of all the times I've hurried home
To see you smiling, standing there,
To see your face, to feel your touch,
To feel your questing kisses roam,
To smell the perfume of your hair,
The sweetheart that I love so much.

✻❤✻

Come, My Love!

Come, my love, let's steal away
On quiet paths along the shore
With Douglas firs, where eagles soar
And walk and talk - and thrill me.

Come, my love and hold my hand
And let me feel your fingers glide
Across my arm and, deep inside,
I glimpse a wonder-land.

Come, my love and dance with me
And let me see your eyes, alight
With love and warm and deep delight,
Caress - and yes - seduce me.

✳❤✳

Moon over Lasqueti   R. Cain

Moonlight Love

I woke. Your hair was bathed in moonlight,
Your breathing, soft as summer air;
Your shoulder, softly-silvered, shining
And, oh - I loved you, lying there.

❋❤❋

Songs of the Sixties

Your lips entice, your eyes entrance,
Your arms around my neck, we dance
To songs of love, a broken heart,
Stars and moonlight, constancy
And anguish when apart.

What fun to feel the drive, the sound,
These songs I share with you,
To feel those hormones bounce around,
The way they ought to do!

✳❤✳

THE BIRDS AND THE BEES

✳❤✳

The Foxgloves

Two foxgloves nodding in the breeze,
One, purple, elegant and tall,
The other, dressed in bridal white
And meadow green, that's all.

She bows her head so shyly,
He leans across to kiss,
A purple petal falls to earth,
A sign of foxglove bliss.

The Song of the Bees

The bees hum a lullaby, lilting for lovers,
In the heat of a summery, still afternoon;
Each wingbeat a note in a symphony, hovers,
A delicate part of an intricate tune.

Singing of sunshine and flowers in profusion
Bedecking the sward on the slope of the hill,
Forming a carpet of coloured confusion,
Laying down memories, lingering still.

✳❤✳

A Giant to the Rescue

We think of the bee with its lifetime in hours,
Not much when compared to our seventy years;
In reality, bees are as old as the flowers,
With an ancestry very much older than ours.

Crash-landed and stranded, it wanders around,
Who can imagine its primeval fears,
While the ants call their comrades relentlessly round
For the feast, from their burrows there, deep in the ground.

But the bee, with a vestige of will to survive,
Takes the twig that is proffered, a giant interferes,
With some honey, the bee sips, its muscles revive,
Gathers strength for the journey back home to the hive.

I watch for a minute - it suddenly flies
And is lost, just a speck in the summery skies.

Oi Bee An Immigrant, Oi Bee

Bee see
B.C,
Bee like,
Bee stay.

Me see
B.C.,
Like bee,
Me stay.

♥

The Entomologist-Slash-Apologist

I've never seen a flea with housemaid's knee
Or a louse with a raging bunion,
Or a fly with a sty in his compound eye
Or a wart like a soft-boiled onion;
Nor a bee on a rose with a stuffed-up nose
Nor a wasp with appendicitis
And please tell my why the dragonfly
Never suffers from peritonitis?

I expect that you'll say, in your critical way,
The results of this survey are cooked
And then throw a fit when I simply admit
- The fact is - I can't say I've looked!

✳❤✳

NATURE, COMETS, ECLIPSES AND THINGS

Quebec   R.Cain

Quebec

Trees in burning gold and red, and brilliant green,
A rushing torrent, rocky cliffs, a peaceful lake,
A sight as lovely as I've ever seen,
La Tuque, in late October, that's Quebec!

Yet, on many trucks and vans displayed to view
Upon the flatbed, on the hood, a severed neck,
A sight more horrid than I ever knew,
A moose, in late October, that's Quebec!

Soon the driving snow and cutting cold
Transforms the country, turns the lakes to sugared cake,
Again, a sight quite lovely to behold,
Awaiting spring, in April, that's Quebec!

✳❤✳

The Song of the Rhododendron

As I am a rhododendron
I love all this summery rain,
The cooling breeze and the dampness
Refresh me again and again.

You *may* think I'm greening with envy
Of cactuses out in the sun!
Not me, when the temp'rature 's thirty-five C
I feel just a bit over-done!

Now my leaves are all smooth and all shiny,
My flowers lasted ages and well;
I hope it's like this in September, too,
With a fresh, wet and earthily smell.

I'm sorry I seem to be selfish,
But there's an advantage for you -
My green little buds will be wonderful blooms
In the fullness of next springtime, too!

Hyakutake, 1996   R.Cain

Wasted Journey

Hyakutake (HK)
Was thousands of years on the way
And when she comes back
On this heavenly tack
She may find *we've* wandered away!

❤

A Tail of Two Comets

Hyakutake, without or with sake,
Was a much finer sight
Than Halley's de-light!
It lasted much longer,
Was many times stronger
Than feeble old Halley
Who chose not to dally
And couldn't have brightened
the narrowest alley!

Halley had beckoned since I was a boy;
My fondest imaginings - a sought-after joy.
When that was a failure, a positive dud,
My normal exuberant spirits went "thud"!

When Halley comes next I'll have folded my tentie
Though I *could* be a sprightly one-hundred-and-twenty!
But when HK returns after nine thousand years
What will remain of our hopes and our fears?

One thing's quite certain, I'm sure you'll agree,
I won't be concerned about pains in my knee!

❋♥❋

Comet-watch

The weather had been cloudy
So it came as a surprise
To come out of the movies
To clear and starry skies.

The driving home was easy,
The road was pretty dry,
But the sight that I remember
Was in the western sky:
The moon was low, a crescent,
With the old moon in her arms
And Venus in her beauty
Displayed her brilliant charms;
And there, Hyakutake
With her dim and magic train -
And many thousand years will pass
Before they meet again.

And all our little crises
Will have vanished, like the snow,
But someone will be watching
For the comet's ghostly glow.

And perhaps that someone
Will be like you and me,
Holding hands and watching,
Marv'ling at those three
Reflected in the water,
So calm and very still
And with the welcome lights of home
Behind us on the hill.

Hale-Bopp, 1997   R.Cain

Phantom Eclipse

We jostled at the windows, then went out into the night
To see the earth eclipse the moon - a quite unusual sight
And, sure enough, the show began just after half past four
(I'd set the clock just after four, had time to spare and more).

The moon was swiftly darkened as the shadow swept across,
The stars sprang into brightness - I first saw Cygnus' cross,
Corona Borealis and Arcturus, bright, beside
And there was Hale-Bopp, shimmering, a million furlongs wide,
With stars, like diamonds, all a-glittering in her ghostly tail,
Its brightness almost tangible, a rich and queenly veil.

A violent noise, the clock just rang at five, not half past four!
I woke at once and found my clothes and slippers on the floor.
I threw my clothes on, rushed outside, with dawn not far away,
But, blessedly, the clouds were thick and threateningly grey!

I'd watched the moon eclipsing while sound asleep in bed
And Hale-Bopp was a phantom, trailing diamonds, in my head.

✳❤✳

The Refuge

Oh, I have heard the east wind blow,
From gust to gust, to sleep;
Or, worried, watched Orion go,
His 'customed watch to keep.

I've walked those woods where ogres lurk
And menace in the gloom,
Where conflagrations light the murk
And horrid dangers loom.

But,
There is a place within your mind
Where peaceful waters flow,
A refuge from the daily grind,
Where you can learn to go
To sunlit uplands decked with flowers,
Where sparkling snowfields gleam,
'Neath harvest moon and April showers,
The essence of a dream.

A shelter from all aches and pains
Where sweetest songs are sung,
Where gentle summer always reigns
And we are ever young.

PS: It's easy to rhapsodize, advertise, soliloquize
       On this quietest of spots in your mind,
       But when you're depressed, obsessed or just stressed,
       It isn't that simple to find!

Storm at Phipps Point, Hornby Island   R.Cain

Beastly Storm

When you hear a storm at night,
Raging in the trees,
It doesn't seem remotely like
A gentle summer breeze,
But, rather, like an animal
Howling, mad with pain,
Longing for the solace of
A pleasant summer rain.

Clawing at the windows
And wrenching at the locks,
A screaming, slavering, savage, beast
Our fragile dwelling mocks.
"Just WAIT!", he screams, "My brother comes,
Once in a hundred years,
Buildings breaking, matchwood making,
Fulfilling all your fears!"

✳❤✳

WAR AND REMEMBRANCE

✳❤✳

Flanders

Flanders, where the young men died,
Three hundred every single hour,
A 747 with no survivors
      Every single hour
      Of every day
      Of every year
For four interminable years.

Flanders, when the mothers cried,
Three hundred every single hour,
Women left as sad survivors.
      A generation's flower
      Just swept away.
      They disappear
And leave interminable tears.

A Newly-discovered Grave from 1917 - near Arras

The skeletons, peacefully, lay side by side,
Shoulder to shoulder, placed with pride
   And tender and comradely care.

Some boots, some badges, some scraplets of hair,
An arm, a leg, just lying there,
   An ankle - and nothing much more.

Barely a trace of the tunics they wore
In the battle's heat, in the cannons' roar,
   Just nothing for sweetheart or wife.

Young men all, all wrested from life,
In terror, filth and bitterest strife,
    In springtime, the last they would see,
    Believing the world would be free,
    While the generals chat, over tea.

❤

Daffodils and Death in Kosovo

The stillness of the daffodils, so elegant each spear,
Captures my attention, on an evening, blue and clear,
While, far away, the dogs of war spread death, destruction, fear.

A million people flee their homes, in terror as they go;
We watch their flight, in disbelief, the mountain paths, the snow,
In twos and threes, then multitudes, in columns, winding, slow.

In ruined homes, just shattered walls, the rats and shadows play;
The soldiers strut, and burn, and laugh, in arrogant display
While treasure, unimagined, spills unheeded every day.

The refugees, the empty eyes, the tears, the furrowed cheeks,
An anguished mother mentions losses, trembling as she speaks,
Separated from her sons, her husband, several weeks.

I see narcissi glowing and I hear the robin sing
While men of war, in foolishness, despoil this lovely Spring.

❤

Kosovo Peace Plan

Milosevic just doesn't care how much we bomb his land,
Destroy his infrastructure and his armouries as planned!
It all comes down to money and he knows, when all this stops,
We'll pay for all the damage and replace his wasted crops.
He'll still be hero to the Serbs, retain his tyrant's power
Though Kosovo lies wasted and her folk a shrivelled flower.

The refugees won't all come back, to that extent he wins;
The land is worthless, Serbs move in,
                                        he's wreathed in ethnic grins!
Each minute that the war goes on, vast treasures simply flee,
Washed down with floods of mothers' tears,
                                        down to that sunless sea.

If, first, we'd offered money, he'd have come around real quick;
We should have known this all along - the carrot beats the stick!

Two points of View

Burning houses tell their tales
Of hamstrung hopes and dreams destroyed
While politicians prattle - and generals' sabres rattle
And their spokesmen have their spinning wheels deployed.

✳❤✳

Lest We Regret

Desensitize your children, teach them how to kill!
The violence seen on television - the perfect poison pill!

How many acts of violence? (How many grains of sand?)
Just stop and think how violence warps the children of this land!

Blood, raw sex and horror, are nightly movie fare!
Our children learn that that's OK! It's deadly doctrinaire!

Strike back at violent movies! Their insidious pollution
Of hearts and minds of little kids - and here's a great solution:
Refuse to watch these movies! Refuse to go along!
Write, complain about this crap - it's gone on far too long!

�֍❤�֍

To me, this next poem took on an extra significance
on the death of Princess Diana,
just five days after the poem was written.

Death's Bright Angel

"Think for a moment and tremble, you fool!
Your summers are numbered, alas!
The deeds of your passing are perilous few
- simply tracks on the dew-wetted grass.
All your life's mystery, soon will be history;
Sweet, simple pleasures, like hot buttered bread,
Will cease to be treasures the moment you're dead!"
    Says Death's Bright Angel, beckoning,
    With shining, golden hair,
    While she tallies up your reckoning
    On a gleaming, golden chair.

Then think for a moment and tremble, you fool!
Make the most of each mile of the race
Or you'll stand there before her, transfixed with regret,
As the veil falls, concealing her face.

✳❤✳

Tears and Remembrance - Princess Diana

I don't want to hear of her death in the dark,
See the blood on the wreck of the car,
Hear the horror of crying as life ebbed away
And the portals of Death creaked ajar.

Tears for the sons she was leaving behind,
Tears for the lover who'd died,
Tears for the years that were never to be
- It isn't surprising she cried.

I will remember her, radiant, young,
Soft-focus, a smile on her face,
When she came down the aisle with her prince on her arm,
Demure and so lovely, with sweet, girlish charm,
In rich, silk-caparisoned grace.

✳❤✳

9/11 Tragedy - and a Promise

In dreams, disturbed, and wakefulness,
We share the terror, feel the pain,
The anguish of the hostages,
Trapped aboard each speeding plane.

A woman in her sky-high office
Turns, admires the morning sky,
A hurtling aircraft fills her vision,
She sees she is about to die.

Flame roars through the peaceful office;
Men, machines are swept away,
Roasted, melted, vaporized;
Steel columns soften, burning clay.
In floors above the fiery impact,
The stairwells blocked by fire below,
Roof access doors are barred and locked;
No place to flee, no place to go.

The structure shivers, smoke pours forth,
Tortures lungs and blots the sky,
With dreadful pace the building crumbles
And in the streets the firemen die.

You men of evil, who destroyed
A hundred thousand dreams today,
Before the wrath of God, you'll tremble;
We, or God, will make you pay.

Two Sides of Time - 11 March 2004

I celebrate a hole in one,
Drinks all round and celebration,
Re-live the shot, imagination,
A soaring ball, the morning sun.
Along the shore the herring run,
The sea a milky blue sensation,
Gulls in raucous competition,
Springtime's dance of life begun.

And in Madrid the bombers strike,
The carnage bursting through each train,
Bloody death and horrid fears
Affecting old and young alike.
Millions of marchers in the rain
And Spain awash in tears.

✳❤✳

WEDDINGS AND RETIREMENTS

✳❤✳

A Wedding by Lake Ontario

A shady dell, sun-dappled trees,
A luscious, languid, summer breeze,
    The blue and limpid lake beyond;
Soft melodies from sylvan strings,
A flash of light on swallows' wings,
    The scene is set, our hearts respond.

The bridegroom, tall and somewhat gauche,
Sees his gentle bride approach,
No veil to hide the sparkling eyes,
The rounded cheeks,
The parted lips,
That certain wanton eagerness we always recognize.

The solemn vows, the ring exchange,
The looks young lovers interchange
In Love's delusion's private world
Where everything is sweet and new,
Where troubles are, they're troubles few
And only phantom fears.

We see them through an older lens
And wish their urgent innocence
Would last at least a thousand years.

♥

Wedding Day Hiccup

Great-grandfather died back in nineteen-oh-four
But his teaspoons were sparkling like new!
Professionally polished, individually wrapped
In a cloth of a bright, pretty blue.

Marked with "M" for "McClung" - the old family name -
Her grandma had used them as well -
At soirées, at dinner or tea on the lawn -
Just think of the tales they could tell!

They've heard many secrets in confidence told,
Tales of triumph and tragedy, too,
Soft whispers of love, exclamations of joy
And family hullabaloo!

They now have another sad story to tell
To Kathleen with her bright chestnut hair,
How I went to our car just to fetch her her gift
And found that the spoons weren't there!

And so - I'd forgotten the gift for the bride -
Next morning, 'twas my turn to gloat,
For those silly old spoons were indeed in the trunk
In a bag, hidden under Jane's coat!

✳❤✳

Margaret's Wedding - 3 August 1996

Another little niece gets married;
Not so long ago, it seems,
She lay sleeping in her cot
And smiling in her baby dreams.
    Nothing knowing,
      Not just snowing,
Ottawa had freezing rain!

Once we had a Christmas party,
All my sons, some nephews, nieces;
Margaret gave a piercing scream -
My wineglass shattered, all in pieces!
    No wild dream -
      One high-pitched scream -
I hope she won't do *that* again!

One summer worked at Capilano
Golf Club 'fore she met her Chad,
Started playing golf and soon
She's playing better than her Dad!
    Notwithstanding
      Happy landing,
Her iron shots are still her bane!

Not surprising, she played soccer,
Rallied on by Al and Jim;
Spent some years at UBC -
BA in Hist'ry, on a whim.
    Fluent talker,
      Dropped her soccer,
Now plays softball with her swain.

She's been known to play the market,
Bought some Starbucks shares, one day;
A lady with her own opinions,
'Though her Daddy told her "Nay"!
    Profit gaining,
      Sweet champagning,
Dad's laments were quite profane!

✳❤✳

With Chad she wandered to Australia
(On our planet's darker side?)
Works hard - but took a day's vacation -
Standing here - a smiling bride!
   As we kiss her
   We all wish her
Happiness may never wane.

A Wedding Limerick

Now Stephen and Krista are wed,
There are many things better unsaid,
   Though their eyes may be glist'ning,
   They're really not list'ning,
They're longing to leap into bed!

James McGhie and Sarah Newton Manson

Grandpa's Wedding - July 1901

I see their wedding photo
So formal and so grand,
His top-hat, gloves, so firmly in his hand;
Her dress a ribbed creation
In organdie and tulle
And billowed hat, her figure like a wand.
I wonder if he'd held her hand, or if he'd ever kissed her?
I wonder if she called him "Jim", or if she called him "Mister"?
Their gazes duly steady,
Their solemn vows so new,
Their marriage still a hazy, dreamy vista.

❤

Stuart Lang's Retirement

His talents he honed in a mill in Brasil
Where the hemlines were tied to inflation;
He modernized Skookumchuck, boiler and all,
And dabbled in power generation,
But the cream of the crop was a bright modern mill,
His Alberta-Pacific creation.

He's broad in the beam and as broad in the grin
And quick with a humour injection,
But if you were the target of Stu's steely eyes
Or a statement disguised as a question
You couldn't start bluffing - he'd have you on toast,
Tenderized, grilled to perfection!

To hand on the torch isn't easy to do,
It's an age-old and wrenching requirement.
We're sure that his interests will soften the blow -
Raise your glasses to Stuart's retirement!

✳❤✳

Phlying Phil Phinally Retires

He's not exactly tall and slim
No unassuming cherubim,
When he was born his size and weight - one only can surmise -
But it seems to me he's always been this size!

St Albans saw his early years
His early hopes and boyhood tears
At sweet sixteen he went to sea to earn his daily bread
And the Navy took him sailing round the Med.

At twenty, Phil was back on land
And turned his myriad-minded hand
To Cost and Works Accountancy, which seemed an easy job
Then Pat turned up and caused his heart to throb!

In nineteen-fifty-four they wed
(You had to then, to get to bed!)
Toronto saw him working sev'ral months as chief cashier
But he left - I think he didn't like the beer!

Then Winnipeg Supply and Fuel
Hired our hero, this shining jewel,
And he was now in sales, a job he'd wanted since a boy
And cricket was his leisure-time employ.

'Twas then that wicked ECA
Enticed our Phlying Phil away;
Then Diamond Blowers, Calgary, next step in his career;
Then Babcock hired him - they had cause to cheer!

His dedication, none outshine -
Once, he had trouble with his spine;
With clients breathing down his neck, to keep the job on track,
Phil read setting drawings lying on his back!

Babcock moved him to Vancouver,
For Phil and Pat, a great manoeuvre -
In Chilliwack, kept ducks and hens, a jolly coterie
And steers called T-bone One, and Two, and Three!

Phil's always been a party guy
Who loves to drink the bottle dry;
La Crêperie, but, late one night, he nearly caused some strife
He was dancing on the table with my wife!

In meetings Phil can do his stuff,
For clients, just cannot do enough!
I'm sure he has a thousand friends - and I can tell you why -
He's a much more diplomatic man than I!

As well as his diplomacy -
He's got a super memory
Not just for Babcock clientele, but folks like you and me;
And he's friendly, warm and jolly, you'll agree.

So now that Phil's retirement's here
We'll miss this boiler buccaneer
- Perhaps a budding charioteer -
Five hundred years from now I see Phil Heighton riding high
On a great big Babcock boiler in the sky!

I see him soar with stainless wings
All reinforced with tubes and things
And, circling round, hear how he sings
Round ABB in dazzling rings!
One final thought to dissipate such dreams of sad revulsion -
He'll be using Diamond blowers for propulsion!

❤

A Babcock Party - Terminal City Club, Vancouver

This spring invitation brought joyous elation -
How could we ever refuse
A Babcock spring party - it may not be arty -
But the food's great and so is the booze!

It's a chance to say "Hi!" to this or that guy
You never would otherwise see
You'll get up to date and it won't finish late -
It's quite a respectable spree!

It gives us the chance, without having to dance,
To gab about boilers and steam,
About gaskets and handholes and full-access manholes
And asbestos - the boiler-man's dream!

Some people will say, in an underhand way,
This poem 's an ad for my book,
That I'm only wangling and cleverly angling
To reel in a few on my hook!

No - I must deny such a horrible lie
As I stand here enjoying my wine,
The picture of Innocence, if not of Abstinence,
Having a wonderful time!

We're birds of a feather who've gathered together -
Raise your glasses and cheer, as of yore!
The goodies you bite on are thanks to Phil Heighton
Mike Trivett, Eliz'beth and more!

Cheers!!!

❋♥❋

The Engagement of Sophie Rhys-Jones and Prince Edward:
Her Dad's Perspective

They're a very handsome couple,
But, since I'm her loving father,
The last five years have seemed an age,
I've worked up quite a lather!
To think that, maybe, Edward,
HRH, and clever,
Was just another fly-by-night
- Or fly-by prince, whatever!

I know his Mum's respectable,
Perhaps a bit aloof,
But I worry 'bout the goings-on
Beneath the palace roof!
Its darkened grandeur, late at night,
With all that that entails,
Even if his brother
Is the Prince of ruddy Wales!

His Grandpa - King of England -
His father, something else,
His Grannie comes from Scotland,
- But, at least their dogs are Welsh!
I think of press exposure,
Of each reporter's moan;
- I hope the Poet Laureate
Will leave them both alone!

He's got a decent job in films,
I like the royal name,
But Sophie's clock is ticking,
So I worry, just the same.
I'm pleased to see them so relaxed,
I know her happy smile,
But I won't be feeling quite at ease
'Til he takes her down the aisle.

A TOUCH OF BURNS

Robert Burns Night At The Vancouver Rowing Club

A roomful of Scotsmen all chattering there,
Convivial drinking,
Congenial thinking -
Burns would have loved it -
The food and the friends,
The warmth of the company making amends
For the toil of the week.
The jokes, tongue in cheek,
Hyperbole, Scottish and typical -
Just joking and not hypocritical!

My very first visit was fun-filled and frisky
Especially when
One of the men
Drew out my name from the hat!
How about that!
A glittering bottle of fine Scottish whisky!

Vancouver   R.Cain

Horror - of Burns

I suppose I awoke from the sound of the flames
Or the noise of our neighbours all shouting our names!
     In the instant of waking -
     What a row they are making -
     Air smoky and bright -
     Light filling the night!

As I leap to my feet from my somnolent daze,
Through the window I see the whole hillside ablaze -
     Fire raging and white -
     Brilliant pinpoints of light -
     Fire to the eaves
     Silhouetting the leaves
     In the curtain of fire
     Raging higher and higher!

     Oh God! Please have pity!

Yes - it was only the lights of the city -
Vancouver, the traffic, the noise of the night -
To me from my island - oh, Lord - what a fright!

A Touch of Burns

It was suggested recently
That Burns is in my family tree
And I'll relate how that might be,
    So gather round
And listen quiet and patiently
    Without a sound.

At Bogwood Toll there lived a maid,
Bright and blithe, not dull and staid,
She captivated Burns, who said
    He'd get the lass
And cuddle her beneath his plaid
    Upon the grass.

But, alack, the lass was wed
And shared the blacksmith's marriage bed.
His name was Manson, his nose was red
    And veined with blue.
He'd waked wi' mony an achin' head
    Still partly fu'.

And George, the smith, was big and brawny,
Wi' hands like shovels, gnarled and bony,
He'd been known tae lift a pony
    For a shilling.
He had a fear that his wee honey
    Was somewhat willing.

And so he watched her like a hawk,
Sae bonny in her summer frock.
He didnae like to see her walk
    Wi' Burns's ilk -
Sae fu' o' charm and gentle talk
    An' tongue o' silk.

※❤※

Now Janet, who'd been married young,
Was charmed by Rabbie's golden tongue,
Admired him as he walked among
        The fields o' rye
And mony bonny smiles he flung
        Tae catch her eye.

As mentioned, George was wont tae drink
Until his eyeballs mellowed pink,
His coins he'd on the counter clink
        And order more
Till he couldnae speak and barely think -
        Sat on the floor.

The pub was Poosie Nancy's place,
Right by the kirkyard's sombre grace
Where tall trees' branches interlace
        In Mauchline town
Where simple drink brought nae disgrace
        Nor chiding frown.

So, one winter's eve and raw,
The rain and sleet were near tae snaw,
But there, in Poosie Nancy's ha'
        'Twas warm and cosy
And George an' Rab an' Johnnie a'
        Wi' ale were rosy.

When came the witchin' hour at nine,
George was drunk, but Rab was fine,
By accident, or by design
        He helped George home -
Where Janet sat, her eyes a-shine -
        A 'witchin' poem.

✳❤✳

Janet, in the kitchen, tended
Their happy home, the while she mended
A pile of socks that never ended,
          Wi' hot resentment
While George his wayward homeward wended
          In warm contentment.

Though Janet sat there, quite forlorn, she
Kept her husband's dinner warm, she
Put a pretty apron on, she
          Arranged her hair;
If she had known that Rab was raunchy,
          She'd taken care!

Somehow George got up the stair
Wi' help frae Rab an' Janet there
And far beyond all pain an' care
          He fell asleep;
Left Rab an' Janet, happy pair,
          A tryst tae keep.

Janet offered Rab a dram
A piece o' bread, a slice o' ham,
Topped it off wi' home-made jam,
          Sweet turtledove!
Rab sat an' ate an' didnae sham
          His looks o' love.

Janet found her thoughts a-swither,   *in a whirl*
Here they were, the two, thegether;   *together*
One kindness swiftly brought anither
          And, nine months later,
Wee Alex had a little brither
          - A hot potato!

✳❤✳ 82 ✳❤✳

✳♥✳

The lad, called John, became a tailor,
Nae blacksmith boy nor wandrin' sailor,
Nor captain o' a Boston whaler
    - A slender laddie -
Nae giant, leerie wifie-hater   *suspicious*
    Like George, his "Daddy"!

And George was never party to
The secret only Janet knew;
She watched one grandson as he grew
    - Wee James, not Gerald -
Become the music critic to
    The Glasgow Herald.

James wrote songs, a book o' lyrics
Of roses, love among the hayricks,
Elegies an' panegyrics
    In noble tone.
Auld George had surely had hysterics
    Had he but known!

Coincidence, all this may be,
But farther down the family tree,
There came another poet, me,
    Nae care harasses -
Wi' songs an' rhymes an' lightsome e'e
    For bonny lasses.

Note: The above poem about the Mansons has the same
rhyming construction as many of Robert Burns' poems and
as the said James Manson's poem "Happy Geordie" on
page 366 of his book "Lyrics and Ballads" published by
David Robertson in Glasgow, in 1863. James, born in
1809, was 54 years old then. He was my great-grand-
uncle.

❤

Robert Burns' Season Again
(Tune: "Phil the Fluter's Ball")

With his fires, and desires, and the twinkle in his eye,
Robert Burns was quite a character, I cannot tell a lie!
To a Louse, To a Mouse, to the lark up in the sky,
But the poems I love the most are those that tend to make me cry!

Songs serene, sweet poteen,
        O how green they grow, the rashes, O!
The poem o' the daisy that he crushed among the stour,
Quick verse, sharp verse, to wicked verse was no' averse,
And lovely songs of love he wrote to every paramour!

He was brash, he was rash, ever fashin' o'er the lassies, O!
Drunk as a skunk, down at Poosie Nancy's bar!
He was great, we relate to his every human failing and
This time of year you hear us sing his praises from afar!

There's the tune, Bonnie Doone, and that lovely Afton Water, O!
I'd miss Ae Fond Kiss and John Anderson, My Jo,
Fair hair, black hair, his out-of-wedlock daughter, O!
The words that ring on down the years evocatively glow!

✳❤✳

POEMS FROM THAT EMERALD ASTEROID - HORNBY ISLAND

Sea Lion Saga

Hark! The Hornby sea lions sing
Of Christmas fast approaching!
They'll be here from now 'til spring
With carefree salmon poaching.
But when a killer whale 's in sight,
You'll hear them go all quiet,
For sea lions make a tasty bite
In every orca's diet!

If I were a bug in a polar-bear rug
In an igloo far north of the tree-line,
I'd dream of disporting, continuous courting,
A libidinous, sinuous sea lion!
If you and I were sea lions here,
We'd swim and dive with pleasure,
With baby sea lions every year
- The fruits of all that leisure!

Primeval Urges
(The Lambert Channel - March)

In the moonlight, hear them barking,
Coughing, grunting, gurgle, sniff!
Disembodied sea lions larking,
Or a sea lion lover's tiff!

In the daytime, quietly snoozing,
Tails or flippers in the air,
Gorged from hours of sea lion boozing,
Drunk with herring, free from care!

One, a sentry, at his station,
Barks at me, upon the shore,
A warning or an invitation
To join them on the ocean floor,
To trace the kelp-bed's shadowed mazes,
Glistening, smeared with herring roe,
To surface, where the sunlight blazes,
Sense the ocean's ebb and flow.

Chords of our primeval phases
When we were fishes - long ago.

Horse Sense

One evening at dusk, on our way to the store,
I spoke to my wife, then I suddenly swore,
For into my consciousness then did explode
A shadowy shape at the side of the road,
When, in a flash, to my shock and surprise,
A horse and a rider materialize!

Had I been driving rather faster, blinded by a coming car,
Tragedy had struck that evening, swifter than a falling star.
Blood and bits of bone and windshield,
                              writhing horse upon the grass;
We'd be "dead upon arrival", flattened by a horse's arse.
Rider hurled into the hedgerow, broken bones and half alive,
Or, impaled upon a fencepost - the only creature to survive.

Come now, sweet rider - don't be a jerk!
Use reflectors in the murk!

✳❤✳

The Wine Club Steward's Compensation

I believe I'm a generous steward of wine
Who serves, most discreetly, you'll find,
But I'm careful to listen if you would decline
(It reduces consumption and that suits me fine)
This nectar, this gift to Mankind.

I notice the connoisseurs tasting the stuff
With a swirl, then a swallow, perhaps,
Or a grimace that tells me the flavour is rough,
Or a glare if a drop hits their jacket or cuff
          - I'm never afraid they'll collapse.

And then there are others who'll drink it with vim,
No matter the flavour or taste,
As long as their glasses are full to the brim
They're always so friendly, not stuffy or prim,
          They won't let a drop go to waste.

Now what do *I* get from this menial chore,
Repeating the names till I'm hoarse -
No one remembers the wine that I pour,
Nobody cares if my elbow gets sore
          - I salvage the bottles, of course!

※❤※

The Wine Steward's Report
on the Eve of the AGM and Barbecue

It looks as if our wine consumption's going up and up
Although we've just as many tipplers sipping at the cup!
I forgot to carry forward all the bottles that we had
To start the season in September - was I ever *bad*!
However, I can tell you that we scoffed off twenty-six
Bottles red and bottles white - a quite eclectic mix:
BC wine, US red and some the Aussies made
And some plonk our members brewed
                              that could be lemonade!

Most donated just one bottle, in the year that's gone,
But Audrey Ord and Woodley (Jean) as well as Woollard (Pat)
Gave an extra bottle and I've kept a note of that.
Ken and Muriel carry three and, if you're rather curious,
We drank them at the barbecue
                              - the pace was fast and furious!
I can't close off the books just yet - I'm counting as I write -
We may have six or seven left - who gives a toot tonight!

✳❤✳

Hornby Island Recycling Centre - 20th Anniversary Poem
(To Janet, and Annie, and Everyone's Granny
who helps to make it work!!!)

It's strange how it all came to pass,
In a clearing with weeds and some grass,
This community thing,
Where Recycling is king
That no other centres surpass.

We've come a long way since the days
When our burner emitted blue haze -
We recycle much more
Than we used to, before,
In a myriad different ways.

Now, for plastic and cardboard and tin,
Each has a separate bin;
There's a composting spot
Where the worms like it hot,
Because waste is the Eighth Deadly Sin.

If what's needed is bits for a bicycle,
Or trim for an old-fashioned tricycle,
Plus chintz for a chair,
You'll find it all there!
Dump your fridge if it doesn't make icicle!

Most appealing, I think you'll agree,
Is the store - where everything's free!
Books, magazines, all,
Dresses, long, short or small,
Or a shirt you can wear *après ski.*

Drive through our magnificent gate!
Unload all superfluous freight!
When you've finished all that,
You can stand there and chat!
Happy Birthday, Recycling - you're GREAT!

＊❤＊

Deck-Quake
(at the 1998 Annual Golf Tournament on Hornby Island)
(Tune: "Little Brown Jug")

One evening that we won't forget,
Just before the sun had set.
We were there, a motley crowd,
To cheer the winners, oh so proud!

Chorus:

Ha, ha, ha! You and me!
Sat on the deck, by the rail, you see!
Groan, creak, crash! The timbers crack!
Down came the deck like a heart a-ttack!

The sky was blue, the greens were green,
And Little Tribune's golden sheen
Tempted all and sundry there
To steal a glance at the bathers, bare!

A hundred golfers standing tall,
List'ning closely, one and all,
As all the winners' names were called,
Lovely, homely, short and bald!

There must have been some overweight -
Or maybe overloaded plates -
The deck just gave a creaking sound
Then dumped the party on the ground!

No one hurt, I'm glad to say,
They'll all be back once more to play!
I'm glad the sundeck's proud design
Wasn't one that I'd call mine!

✳❤✳

R.Cain

Back row:
  Tom   Tina   Darlene   Joy   Joan Rosemary Moira
 Durrie Harrison Lashley Takefman Brears Nixon   Armour
Front row: Doris Savoie Hilary Brown Jean Woodley

Our Volunteers

We'd like to thank you, Volunteer,
For every task well done,
For helping out, throughout the year,
Without your help we couldn't run!

You're the ones who raise the money,
Boost our ticket sales,
Smooth ruffled fur with words of honey,
Apologise when all else fails!
Arrange the programmes, move the chairs,
Bake a cake or bun,
Help the artists sell their wares
And, in the process, have some fun!

Encourage others when they stumble,
Pacify the cranks,
Your dedication makes us humble -
So, once again - we offer thanks!!!

❤

The Unknown Artist

The Poetry Board beside the Co-op lets each poet share
His musings, prose or rhyme,
Silly or sublime,
With anyone who comes along
Who loves the rhythm of a song
Or castles in the air.

I pinned three poems of comets there
- poems I thought were swell;
With thoughts I thought profound,
I liked their tuneful sound,
But someone came and took the lot!
Was I the victim of a plot?
By whom? I could not tell.

I must admit annoyance rankled in my jealous heart,
But after sev'ral days
(Fate works in funny ways!)
My faith in Goodness was restored -
My poems were back upon the board,
Enhanced by funky art!

This poem 's to thank that unknown artist,
with his reds and blues,
With planets, comets, stars,
With Jupiter and Mars.
Perhaps I'll never know his name,
To catapult it into fame!
(This guy could also be a dame
Who complements my Muse!)

Thanks, Buddy!

❄❤❄

Hornby Island Co-op   R.Cain

Dear Miss Noticeboard ....

I toss a pebble in a pond,
I whisper to a tree,
I whistle to a windy sky,
Sing love-songs to the sea

I pin my poems on this board
And someone reads them - me!

Millennium Shift on Hornby Island
for those who missed it!

The evening started quietly at something after eight,
Suzanne had phoned to warn us all we'd not to come too late
And soon we sat, with drinks before us,
Enjoying the Hornby Island Chorus
And felt excitement building as their tuneful voices rang.

Some jokes from John and Helen,
Then Carole took the stage
And told of Adam, Eve, and their Creator in a rage
At finding them so steeped in sin and flooded with desire,
You'd think they heard Bonita, sexy, singing "Kiss of Fire"!

Two barefoot girls with twirling lights
Displayed their legs in gauzy tights;
A Maori dance, an old tradition,
A special Hornby Isle rendition
And marked the date by painting glowing zeros in the air.

And then we saw some tango dancing,
Just the thing when you're romancing;
Dan Bruiger danced his partner like a wicked millionaire!

But still we hadn't reached the culmination
Of this very special evening's celebration,
Of entertainment, song and dance
- Each challenging coquettish glance
Of belly-dancers jiggling there
Their charms, their hips and rounded arms
With fascinating movements of each lithe spaghetti spine!
You could almost hear the male contingent gulping down its wine!
The swine!

✳❤✳

Seven stalwart fellows, well-endowed,
Then entertained the raucous crowd.
All dressed the same - at least, to start.
Quite hard to tell them all apart!
Until they tipped the applecart,
While stepping trimly, smiling primly,
Each young Apollo struts his stuff,
While slowly stripping to the buff!
Seven gaudy top hats coyly hiding
What could be called their joy and priding!
The music climax - the lights are bright -
We all await that wondrous sight!
Then - all exposed and loth to linger,
We know each by his little finger,
In that tantalising flash before the hall went black as night!

Truly then, the welkin rang
With shrieks and cheers and whistles -
It sounded like a thousand girls
Upon a thousand thistles
And so a thousand years on Hornby ended in delight!

To usher in a thousand years was strange enough itsel'
But, stranger still, the midnight stroke was on a tiny bell!
A moment's silence duly reigned,
A moment's silence well maintained
And then the plaintive verses rang, of hoary "Auld Lang Syne".

Go now, Stranger, read those words,
They speak of friendships, dear.
Take them in your heart of hearts
And feel the warmth each verse imparts
And hope we'll all be singing them another thousand years.

✴❤✴

Dandelion Dinner

A lady told us dandelions are not the threat they seem,
The flowers can make a tasty dish, sautéed they're a dream!
Done with chopped up peppers,
                    some pine nuts, topped with cheese,
They'd have a gourmet beg for more, down upon his knees!

She said they're full of vitamins, the flowers make lovely wine;
Your skin is tighter, eyes are brighter, positively shine!
So, home we went, we picked a bunch, and did then as she said,
A little bitter, tasty though - and then we went to bed.

And the mem'ry lingered on - I thought on each attraction -
Their flavour, their consistency - we ate them to distraction!
But if I hadn't farted until morning, if you please,
I'd have floated out the window, like a seed upon the breeze!

Ferry home   R.Cain

Home Again!
(Late September - all the tourists have gone!)

Got back to Hornby yesterday, to my island home,
Jet-lagged, sand-bagged, from across the foam.
First impressions: very green, leaves a yellow-gold,
Watching from the ferry as the vistas all unfold.

Co-op shopping, empty now, lots of friendly smiles,
Stop and chat to many people in the friendly aisles -
Then the mail - it's in a basket - piles and piles and piles!

Not like Spain, stray cats a-pooping, dogs with frantic yelps;
I imagine salmon sporting, silent, swishing, gently-waving kelps
Night so still, there's nothing stirring - hard of hearing helps!

✳❤✳

GOLFING TRIALS AND TRIBULATIONS

Little Tribune Bay, Hornby Island   R. Cain

Golf - Game of the Gods

Soft grass underfoot and the sun on our face,
Nature's beauty each step while we play,
Exquisite pleasures arise when the ball
Unerringly speeds on its way.

The turn of the shoulder, the sweep of the arm,
The swing of the smooth follow-through
The flight of the ball hanging high in the air,
A diminishing dot in the blue;

The sight of the ball as it falls to the green
And lands a few feet from the pin,
The music the ball makes on hitting the cup
As a twenty-five-footer rolls in;

Even a drive when the ball's in a pond
Is a bitter-sweet pleasure we know,
As long as the shot had that sweetness we crave
In this game of the gods, here below!

❤

Golfing at Little Tribune

Quite often we can hit a par,
Occasionally birdies,
But holes in one are few and far,
As scarce as hurdie-gurdies!

As I hit off from Number One
Across that deadly hollow,
How Nixon yelled, I caught my breath,
- I'd nearly hit a swallow!

Golfing Tips

Determination, concentration, steady follow-through,
A little application and you'll be a golfer too!
Above all else, avoid temptation,
Shun your partner's adulation.
Curb your fanciful ambition,
Down the fairway lurks contrition.

One day you hit an eighty-six - what joy!
Next day you score a hundred - then - oh boy!
Altercation! Desperation! This game can never pall
- Though sometimes you'll admit you'd like to kill that ruddy ball!

✳❤✳

Golf at Little Tribune Bay
(Hornby Island's 4th Annual Golf Tournament)
(Tune: "Has Anybody Seen My Gal?")

One-hundred-and-one
Yards of fun,
That's Peter Wardle's Number One,
Has any-body seen my ball?
One-seven-eight -
Two's just great,
Water on the left and a shed in wait -
Has any-body seen my ball?

And when you're through, with Number Two,
Covered in burrs
One more ball, grass so tall
This sure ain't a course for a-ma-teurs!

Hook on Four!
How I swore -
One ball drowned, must buy some more!
Has any-body seen my ball?
Five - the pond!
The green's beyond!
I hang my head in deep despond!
Has any-body seen my ball?

And if you add your score, to Number Four
Your strokes for Five
Golf's a game - and you're to blame -
You can bet your sweet life that you'll survive!

And last comes Six,
Same old tricks!
One more ball just got deep-sixed!
Has any-body seen my -
Has any-body seen my -
Has any-body seen my ball?

✳❤✳

Opportunity Knocked on Saturday 3 June 2000
on the Fourth Hole at Little Tribune Bay, Hornby Island

Of the thousands of golfers much better than me,
Not many are having such fun,
Where they might contrive just to sink it in three,
- I managed to hole it in one!

Exchanging my sporran, my brogues and my kilt
For practical, light Tilley togs,
While struggling to master my feelings of guilt
As I played in my old Swedish clogs.

The ball was a Top-Flite, a sweet Number 1,
Deep orange and bright as the day;
I'd found it on Tuesday, it glowed like the sun
In the bushes by Little Trib. Bay.

Now I must confess that I've just had a thought
(The connection perhaps is ethereal?)
But I could attribute that wonderful shot
To my golf clubs, or even a cereal!

Versification to me is a "must",
Rhymes rattle around 'neath my tonsure.
This poem you'll find, has a mercen'ry thrust
- I'm now actively seeking a sponsor!

✻❤✻

POEMS WITH A SMILE

R. Cain

Dear-dear, Deer

I had some fine geraniums, each in a pretty pot,
All tended through the winter in a sunny, sheltered spot.
        One night when I retired
        I forgot to close the wire
And, sometime in the light of dawn, the deer devoured the lot!

I've tried so many deer-proof plants, the list is long and fat
And it's extremely detailed - but that means diddly-squatt!
        The compiler 's not to blame,
        Deer eat them all the same
- The young ones just don't read the list as carefully as that!

They gnaw at hawthorn, chew at laurel, eat your garden's pride;
When I've seen the havoc wreaked, I sometimes nearly cried!
        Some people love their grace,
        While others like their face,
I like my deer as venison - smoked, or grilled, or fried!

Albert J. Savoie, off Hornby Island   R.Cain

※❤※

Ferry of Choice

Varied are the vessels of the B.C. Ferries,
Colourful and handsome in their white, blue, red,
With their cargoes of trucks and cars and people
Heading for the places in the net-work spread.

Ferries like the Klitsa on the sail to Coupar,
Carrying the Penelakut - mums, dads, lads,
Then dropping at Thetis, housewives, shoppers,
Sometimes even Scotsmen in their bright-squared plaids.

Serving Hornby Island, and with twin blue smokestacks,
Winter's Albert J. Savoie can dip, yaw, sway,
Though it may be blowing, it never, ever, falters,
Fighting through the spindrift and the wild, blown, spray.

Sailing from Vancouver on the Queen of Surrey
Cruising to Nanaimo with its pine-green strand,
Obstructed by log booms, tug boats, fish boats,
Sail boats in a welter as we near dry land.

High-speed ferries - forty knots and mini bow wave,
Beauty, grandeur, challenge and a short, swift, trip -
Are of value to business- , premium-paying-travellers,
While folk that have the leisure choose a quiet, slow, ship.

Ferries are the backbone of the Island lifeline,
Safe, essential service that we hope will stay
So we must be sure that with the high-speed ferries
The fares stay at a level that we *all* can pay.

PS: Those high-speed ferry elephants
            Were white as the driven snow;
            We sold all three for peanuts
            - *That's* where our taxes go!

✳❤✳

Legal Dispute

Six months is but a lawyer's heartbeat,
A ripple is a raging sea,
A morsel, an outrageous surfeit
So, at least it seems to me!

A molehill soon becomes a mountain,
A matchstick, soon a yarding-pole,
A tiny leak, a jetting fountain,
Your money pouring down a hole!

Each letter, lots of legal jargon,
Each file becomes a hefty tome,
Alas, you'll see no Resolution
'Til all the ruddy cows come home!

Just Another Misunderstanding

One sultry night, she bared her breast
And muttered, in despair,
"I'll go nuts if this goes on,
    I need a little air!"

"Me too!" Her husband then made love
With passion and with flair!
The silly man, he'd got it wrong,
He thought she'd said " - a little heir!"

✳❤✳

The Courts recently supported a lawsuit brought by a couple claiming support from their children. The ruling inspired the following poem:

Admonition to Our Children

Don't spend your money quite so freely,
Maximize your RSP!
According to the latest ruling
You'll end up supporting me!

But, smile, my child, it's most unlikely
The courts will make you pay in full
For all the years we fed and clothed you,
Took you to the swimming pool.
Orthodontists, dentists, classes,
Hockey gear, expensive skis,
Tennis rackets, judo lessons -
I'm sure you thought it all a breeze!
Bicycles and books and bedding,
Med'cines for a ticklish cough
And then, that quite expensive wedding
Just to round the whole thing off!

Add it up, add compound interest
For all the intervening years,
Then note, the sum still won't include
The stress of our parental fears!

We're glad that you've been so successful,
The foot's now in the other shoe;
The aging parent's role reversal -
WE'll be coming after YOU!!!

✳❤✳

*To Andrew Motion (the new Poet Laureate)
regarding his poem about the wedding
of Prince Edward and Sophie-Rhys-Jones*

I liked the poem's basic flow,
The contrast that you chose to show:
The silent church, the solemn air,
The dancing dust-motes sparkling there,
The thronging crowd, the ringing fanfare,
The message to the happy pair
With sober strictures we should share
(A trifle pompous, I declare!).

But -
I think you should have taken time
To find a somewhat better rhyme -
"Air" doesn't rhyme with "disappear",
And "pews" and "vows", I can't espouse,
So try again, please, Andrew, dear!

Beautiful Dreamer's Breakfast

Beautiful bacon, you make unto me
A beautiful breakfast with lashings of tea!
Beautiful bacon, eggs, rashers three!
It's a beautiful morning to wake unto thee!

✳❤✳

Changed Days!

In days of yore, 'way long before
The time that I was born,
A woman was a lady fair,
A rose without a thorn,
With more politeness, gentle brightness,
Lots of social graces.
Today we find that door we open
Slamming in our faces.

I like this new equality,
It keeps us on our toes,
But I wouldn't miss the feminist,
The thorn without the rose.

Hard Sell!

When using Swedish toilet paper
I remember an ad so well -
From back in the swinging sixties -
"Only a child will tell"!

maccallu@mars.ark.com

Don't you find that using e-mail
Brings us all together, close,
Not as close as male and female
- But better than the pony post?

✳❤✳

The E-mail Dummy

Looking through my e-mail,
I received a note one day -
"Look out for certain messages -
They'll blow your drive away!"

"WIN A LOVELY HOLIDAY"
Who could want for more?
But if you read the message
Your computer's out the door!

Like a silly sausage,
I passed the message on
And blocked up every server
From Vancouver to St John!

Luckily Jake Hathaway
From LDS, Salt Lake,
Explained I couldn't catch a bug
That easily - thanks, Jake!

So now when I receive a note
That maybe is a bug,
I contact CIACHoaxes,
So I won't look a mug!

Go thou and do likewise!!!
Contact < http://ciac.llnl.gov/ciac/CIACHoaxes.html>

Progress

We used to write the snail-mail way,
Send greetings now and then,
Newsy notes and little cards,
Hand-crafted - with a pen.

Now, somewhat sad it seems to me,
We get our just desserts
When most communications
Are virus (blank) alerts.

Doggerel

Many people buy a dog,
And those that do, I wish them well,
But I'd wish them weller, sweller,
If they'd buy my dogger-el!

Pick up a poem and taste its texture,
Run the rhymes around your tongue,
You'll find they've much more flavour, savour,
Than picking up that doggie-dung!

Peggy O'Neill

I question if Peggy O'Neill was a lady
In one of the songs that I heard, as a kid;
As I recall, she was Queen of Vulgarity
And I remember she did it for charity -
But I'm damned if I know what it was that she did!

✳❤✳

Joanne's Lucia Fest

Festly food and great libations
Contribute to a mirth-day,
But they gave me palpitations
The day before my birthday!

The Thief

Savour those stolen hours of summer
With a book beneath a tree,
But when the clock was changed this morning
Summer stole an hour from me!

Compatibility

It's strange that we can sometimes argue
Over things inconsequential;
Dinner talk can escalate
To anger often exponential.

Passions underneath the surface
Fuel discussion loud and high,
But we reach complete agreement
Eye-to-eye - and thigh-to-thigh!

✳❤✳

A Tale of Two Loves

The book that he lent me, there in my dream,
Was ragged and torn,
The binding was worn,
Published in India, so it did seem,
With poems both glad and forlorn.

There were songs of the exile, remote from his home
With sadness and rage
And notes on each page,
Eloquent, trivia, scribblings from Rome
And things you would never presage.

I read it with pleasure, passionate songs
Of the heat in the plain,
The longing for rain;
The cry for the hearth where the heart still belongs
And of love, sweet, requited, again.

Then, inside the cover, his handwriting there;
He wrote of a girl,
His thoughts in a whirl.
He loved to distraction, was caught in her snare,
Gave her many a ruby and pearl.

How, hard as he'd striven to wake her desire,
She was cool as a lily,
Decidedly chilly.
With bare toleration she'd watch him perspire
And thought him a little bit silly.

Her sadism sated, she gave back the ring,
Supercilious smile.
He grieved for a while,
Found a girl who would love him,
with whom he could sing,
Lived with happiness, passion and style.

The Scotsman's Secret

As a Scot, my lips are sealed,
For I'd be filled with guilt
Should I reveal what Scotsmen wear
Underneath the kilt!

In Canada and USA,
You know us at a glance
Because a Scotsman never wears
The kilt beneath his pants!

Noisy Night

There's someone snoring through the wall;
The reverberations down the hall,
Growling, roiling, rumbling, free,
Remind me of an MGB!

Sister Sally's Shop

Happy Haircutters - Suite 21 -
Will style your hair - it's lots of fun!
Look like a million! Feel like a queen
With a swing in your step like Sweet Six-teen!

✳❤✳

Holy Willie - Him, Him - or You?

Clinton wears his sackcloth well!
Of course he's sorry - you'd be, too,
If you had faced the show-and-tell
Of Monica - and dresses blue!

How silly all the righteous fuss
O'er peccadillos now laid bare!
We're only glad it wasn't us
Attracting all the public's stare!

Holy Willie 's 'live and well,
With Gingrich stuck astride the fence,
While Clinton's ratings rise and swell
- Hoist by people's common sense!

Maybe He Did - Maybe He Didn't

It's interesting to see the spin the pundits push at us.
Consider William Clinton and the current sexual fuss!
They say he's very clever, and if they're to be believed,
If he hadn't been distracted - what might he have achieved?

The Monica Lewinsky thing provided much distraction;
Though Clinton's smart,
                 it must have curbed his presidential action.
The economy has leapt ahead, forever up and up
- Perhaps he didn't have the time to really mess it up!

✳❤✳

Déjà Vu

I've met some crooks, I've met some fools,
But didn't know it then!
They didn't play by any rules
And would have scored a zero on a scale of one to ten!

When in the mail, there comes a tale
Of thousands down the drain,
Of plans de-railed, of mortgage failed,
I get that sinking feeling, thinking, "Here we go again!"

My stomach churns, my heartburn burns,
It isn't really fair,
But nonetheless, the world still turns.
It isn't any wonder that I haven't any hair!

Gents

It struck me, as I rinsed my fingers in that shiny sink,
A useful notice on the wall
Admonishing - both one and all -
"Please stand a whole lot closer
'Cause it's shorter than you think".

♥

Murphy Does It Again!

Murphy guards your deep-well pump
Until one day, it's snowing;
Gives your funny-bone a bump,
Cuts your foot while mowing!

Seals envelopes without enclosures,
Puts splinters in your finger,
Lets slip embarrassing disclosures
When he cares to linger!

Knocks china cabinets over end,
(That one was a bummer!)
Blocks your toilet round the bend -
You have to call the plumber!

He punctures tyres on parking lots
Impregnates your daughter,
Hits, instead of wondrous shots,
New golf balls in the water!

He'll also plug your septic field,
In icy winds and pouring,
But if he wasn't there, I feel -
Wouldn't Life be boring?

❤

Insurance Reminder!

There's many a slip 'twixt the shore and the ship;
A thief can run off with your baggage!
You *could* bash your head on the end of the bed,
Or choke on a morsel of cabbage!

Sprainings and twists can dislocate wrists
And stumbles can damage your ankle;
Montezuma's Revenge is top of the list
To set all your tubes in a fankle.

You could swallow a fly, get grit in your eye,
Take a fall from an elephant prancer;
Then there's a cold from a patch of green mould,
Influenza, or worse, from a dancer!

Travel insurance is really quite cheap,
So how can a'body refuse it?
Get extra insurance and smile in your sleep
- If you're lucky, you won't have to use it!

❤

I Love It

A buddy of mine has a luxury car,
Stylish, not nearly as sporty
And our golf clubs and golf carts won't fit in his trunk
- But they do in my Volvo S40!

It's snazzy and jazzy and runs like a charm,
My image is younger, I know!
The kids at the golf club are envious now
- and it handles so well in the snow.

I know my S40 is safer, by far
And promises much longer life,
For the money my buddy has spent on his car
- Volvos - for me and my wife!

✳❤✳

Morningside - On Quebec
- or -
Quebec! Wake Up!

On Morningside, the other day,
I heard three Montreal Anglos say
That separation's on the way,
    With deep regret.
Bemoaned provincial disarray
And fiscal debt!

Clearly, they were strongly bound
To Montreal, a home they'd found
But feared its fabric was unwound
    By FLQ;
We heard in Gzowski's mellifluous sound,
    He sorrowed too.

All had lived there many years;
All had normal hopes and fears;
At times they seemed not far from tears
    On Gzowski's talk-back.
All would gladly give three cheers
    To turn the clock back.

They talked of the town, of many years past,
Montreal's lively sidewalks - folk having a blast!
Its cultural mixture quite unsurpassed
    Where e'er the winds blew.
A happiness somehow they felt couldn't last -
    Too good to be true.

♥

They spoke of kids who'd moved out west,
Seeking the future with zip and zest;
All were admitting they thought it best,
        With Quebec down the drain.
Bilingual Anglos who'd pass any test
        Were Calgary's gain.

Don't kill the goose! Don't foul the nest!
This country, Canada, is blessed
With riches, cultures - a bequest
        Of brilliant feather!
Quebec, our love, will die unless
        We work together!

To Peter Gzowski, CBC/Morningside

How about a French translation
Broadcast from our fav'rite station?

❤

Role Reversal

I'd carry you over the threshold, my dear,
If only I felt a bit stronger,
But *you're* ninety-two and weigh nearly a ton
- I'm *not* seventeen any longer!

And so, I suggest that I husband my strength
And surrender myself to your arms;
Then *you* carry *me* up the stairs to our room
And sweeten my nights with your charms!

We won't tell a soul that we've interchanged roles;
It's a ploy that we'll secretly treasure.
And so we'll contrive to keep Love's flame alive
And maximize marital pleasure!

✳❤✳

When Democracy Goes Out the Window

I heard a mother in the store, sev'ral days ago,
      Brightly ask her son
"What would you like for dinner, Jason?" -
      Or "Peter", "Paul" - or "Hon.".

I'm sure the little kiddie was at most three-and-a-half
      Maybe nearly four
And, like a child, his mind was only
      Focussed on the store.

How could he ever think ahead as far as dinner-time?
      Wasn't hungry now!
Wanted nice big creamy milkshake
      As big as she'd allow!

And tortellini wasn't what he wanted for his tea,
      Nor was fish or ham!
All he could think of - ice cream milkshake -
      Maybe topped with jam!

The mummy asked the kiddie what he'd like to eat next day
      But he didn't know;
Oranges, apples, peaches, grapefruit,
      But Jason answered "NO"!

Democracy does not apply when shopping for your kids!
      Don't go ask your tot!
Serve up the food - and if he's hungry,
      Just watch him eat the lot!

✳❤✳

La Manga Holiday

Late in October, the nights are quite cool
But the days are deliciously warm;
One day of rain, quite torrential, with wind
And none of the holiday swarm.

La Manga, deserted, no trace of the crowds
That bustle and jostle in June,
Apartments are empty, the restaurants closed,
Clear Mediterranean moon.

Start off the day with a lovely long lie,
A couple of hours at the beach,
Clear, sparkling water, a brilliant blue sky
And an excellent book within reach.

Luncheon at two at Cabo de Palos,
A restaurant right on the sea,
Pricey, but tasty. A fresh autumn wind
Whips the wavelets to cream, running free.

Old Cartagena, pedestrian streets,
A jumble, a warren, a treat,
Children in uniform, running from school,
Laughter and pattering feet.

Ancient amphorae retrieved from the sea,
Roman lead billets, and tin;
Many small people and, sometimes, a dwarf,
Some poverty, absence of sin.

Here were the Romans, Phœnecians, the Turk,
The triremes, the choice of the Greek,
Magnificent harbour, with warships at work,
The castle of Moors on the peak.

Some houses are tawdry, and many run down,
Ruins all badly let go,
The remains of a temple, the wreck of a church
Where the cats and the rank grasses grow.

Clusters of buildings and building sites, dumps
Of "*basura*", waste plastic and cans,   *rubbish*
Swallows and gulls leave no trails in the sky
For the rubbish can only be man's.

A New Green Bathing Suit

In a pretty bathing suit
You're shapely, sexy, even cute!
Vibrant, glad to be alive!
Who would guess you're sixty-five!

What's your secret, tell me, dear?
Not a wrinkle, ear to ear!
Fitting costume, such good taste -
Every bump correctly placed!

Are you this century's Orlando?
What can I, your loving man, do?
I hear the bells of Aging chime
I'm getting older all the time!!!

✳❤✳

My Other Love, Vancouver
(From "Vancouver Playground")

I'd like to keep a little corner of my heart,
A tiny corner just for me,
A little itsy-bitsy corner from the start,
     For my secret lover and me.

Chorus: I don't want brotherly love, don't want motherly love,
I want luverly love from you, my darling
And if you will play, then you can steal me away
     From my other love, Vancouver!

I've met a load of sweethearts who have said that they
All love me for myself alone;
They have to love Vancouver or they're on their way -
     I don't even bother to phone!

So if you really love me and you hold me close
And if our love is meant to be
Then here's a little love triangle I propose
     That's you, dear, Vancouver and me!

Birthday Consolation

Now you have a Care Card;
It's gold, but you are blue!
But in another few short years
I'll have a Care Card too!

✳❤✳

Thanks, Genes!

How can Existence be just an illusion
When much of it, clearly, is painfully true?
In the still of the night, when I'm free from intrusion,
I think of the past that has made me - and you.

Four million years back to all our beginnings,
Ape-like and shambling and covered with hair,
Darkness brought danger and fear for the family,
The leap of the leopard, the bite of the bear.

In dark, sheltered caves in the quiet before dawning,
Or under a rock in the lee of a hill,
Our ancestors planned for the hunt in the morning -
The spears and the gashes, the chase and the kill.

No wonder we worry 'bout death and our taxes,
Getting the groceries and answering faxes!

✳❤✳

Kindred Spirits in the Future

It's curious to think, as I sit here and rhyme
This *could* be read, far in the future,
Perhaps by an astronaut living on Mars,
Or maybe just Willie, the butcher!

This poem may be read while you're resting in bed
With a fractured and fresh-bandaged femur,
Or perched in a tree near to Trincomalee,
Awaiting a glimpse of a lemur!

I write poems for a lark, conjure smiles in the dark,
A guffaw, or a tear from your eyeball
And when I've succeeded, the tonic you've needed
's less fattening, much, than a highball!

I know there are poets, all snobs and they show it,
Who sneer at my rum-titty-tum,
But, as I get older, I shoot from the shoulder
And call a posterior, a bum!

So,
If you're in my future, as Willie the butcher,
King Charlie or President Gore,
Or if you're a couple, with limbs lithe and supple,
A-rolling around on the floor,
Then pick up a rhyme, preferably mine!
We'll connect, if you're smiling once more!

✳❤✳

THE JOYS OF PUBLISHING

Query to a Publisher

O Jordan Fenn, O Jordan Fenn,
Why don't you contact me now and again
And say if you relished the words from the pen
Of the lady who rattled off "Emily", then
We can settle the price
(Now that would be nice!)
Then we'll both make a million, or hopefully, ten!!!

Publishing Pleasures

How can I be sure
That my poems, puce or pure,
(None exactly poor!)
    Will ever sell?

Sentimental I may be,
But I've known since I was three
That two and one make three -
    That's just as well!

In dark moments of despair
I see, underneath my chair,
A thousand copies mould'ring there!
    Oh, bloody hell!

✳❤✳

Advertising Rhymes (for "Mainly Sentimental")

Come, come buy my little book!
It's a beauty, take a look!
Two hundred pages, nicely bound -
Even pictures to astound!
Poems of joy and mirth and gladness,
Some with laughter, some with sadness
- and here and there a touch of madness?

A treat to give yourself or friend -
You'll enjoy it to the end!

A present of this little book
Will please your lover(s)
Sweeten foes;
Even just a casual look
Between its covers
Will banish woes.
Lots of poems are bright and merry
And Sundance stocks it at the ferry!

I know that you'll find that it's really a hellia
Buy to be had at Ford's Cove and Wrangellia!

❤

Letter to The Editor

Dear Sir,
　　　I write to your attention
To get The Globe and Mail to mention
My poems, " Mainly Sentimental",
A title not just accidental:
Two hundred pages, pictures too,
To illustrate some points of view;
Two-fifty poems that rhyme and scan,
Of Love and Life and Fellow Man,
With far more laughs than Margaret Atwood
And many poets not ev'n that good;
Poems polite and some not that rude!

At Coles it's $17.95,
Poems to make you feel alive;
At SmithBooks, Chapters, priced the same,
My shining moment, seeking fame!

For a gift below your Christmas tree,
Send $18.95 to me
On Hornby Island in B.C.,
I'll send it to you, postage free
And pay the dreaded GST.

And if this verse just leaves you miffed,
Remember, poetry is a gift,
A gift to soothe the savage breast,
To woo a maid, to charm a swain,
Come, buy one - put it to the test!

✳❤✳

Book Review - The Raincoast Kitchen

I volunteered a book review
To earn a measly buck or two;
The package came, I took a look -
My God - it was a cookery book!

The Cookbook Committee in Campbell River
Serves research and recipes well mixed together;
Stories of hunters and settlers and pie,
Cooks flapping hotcakes and sizzling fish fry,
Explorers and loggers enjoying their food
In tents and encampments, wherever they could;
Sportsmen and women in summer employment.
The food and the anecdotes both give enjoyment.

This is no ordinary cookery bookery -
It certainly merits a leisurely lookery!

✳❤✳

Soft Sell

I watch you seek the rhythm of the poem as I read
In the busy, crowded market by my stall.
I enunciate and modulate, responding to your need
To be captured and enraptured in its thrall.

Your eyes are green, or blue, or brown, your skin is young or old,
Your lips are lined, or smooth as nectarine,
Waiting, like an infant, for the story to unfold
Like the pattern on a fabric Damascene.

You'll read the poem later and, maybe, who can tell,
You'll remember your reaction there that day;
The words are sweet, seductive and they held us in their spell
- The crowds recede, the bustle fades away.
You see your Grandmas's bedroom, your mother's wavy hair,
You smell the lilac blossom on the air.

✳❤✳

CORN

The Dance of the Snowflakes

If snowflakes went to dancing class,
The dance they'd want to know
Would have to be the Quickstep
- Snow, snow, quick-quick, snow!

Confucius, He Say ....

A Chinese had a tender jaw,
A simple toothache, nothing more.
The tooth came out and then they found
The root was screwed around and round.
Confucius say (this isn't fiction!)
- "Tooth is stranger than affliction!"

Pun It Again!

"The pun is the lowest form of wit"
My English teacher said.
How is it then, that my feet are funny,
But the prawns are in my head?

Lamentable

A paleontologist I once knew,
Erudite and a Jacobite too,
    Could dance and sing so charmin',
Taught evolution, breathed revolution,
    Singing "Charlie is my Darwin"!

✳❤✳

The Magic Toot

In a corner of my cranium
Lies the complex word "geranium";
With one note on my harmonium
It's transformed to "pelargonium"!

Confusion

Now that I'm a little deaf, don't always hear the word,
People say the strangest things, they're verging on absurd.
A chap I spoke to recently, with quite a friendly smile,
He owned two lots on Hornby and he'd had them quite a while;
He said they were contiguous and that one was on the beach
- I nearly then suggested that he sprinkle them with bleach!

Attention!!!

To get my pension 's
My intention
Barring medical intervention
To cure my raging hypertension
Caused by repetitive rhyme invention
And the motive, I might mention
Of seeking a significant life extension -
We're all a long time dead, Ned!
Now I'll quit while I'm still ahead, Fred!

Timely Tip

Reward yourselves for being punctual,
Alarm clocks give a nasty shock,
It's great to be a little early
- Make nooner-time eleven o'clock!

✳❤✳

Just Wondered?

When a man and his wife have a sporty routine
- Callisthenics that neither one shirks -
At the risk of offending, I suppose you could say
They're a couple of physical jerks?

A Jacobite's Lament for Summer 1999

Bonnie summer 's noo awa'
Softly pours unfriendly rain
Wetter, no, ye canna be,
Will ye no' come back again!

Changed for the Better?

I hear people say that the girls of today
Are relaxed, I'm delighted to hear it -
That many young ladies are "loose as a goose"
- In the fifties you never got near it!

The Linguist

As a linguist who loves his food,
With age I'm getting wiser -
I know *côtelette d'agneau* 's a chop,
Hors d'œvres - an appetizer!

Vive la Différence!

You and I have different worries,
So have cats and dogs
And water snakes pose problems, too,
For scrumptious little frogs!

Personal Choice

I won't write verse like Ogden Nash,
I like my poems less fractured,
Though I'm tempted by the thought of all that cash
For composing stuff that's
carefully, cannily, craftily, ill-manufactured!

✳❤✳

The Limerick

A limerick captures a thought,
Like a water-drop into a pot,
Of a dame, an old flame,
Or a moment of shame,
Or one one ought not to have thought!

If you've never read poetry before,
If it rhymes then it isn't a chore
And part of the plan
Is that each line should scan
And then you'll enjoy it much more!

———————

Grammatical Hint

The contraction for "it is" is "it's";
It's *there* the apostrophe fits!
And if you're obsessive,
To form the possessive,
The apostrophe's out - then, it's "its"!

———————

Consolation

The Greenies all holler and screetch,
Global warming is now within reach;
There'll be lots of surprises
When the sea level rises
- Our house will be right on the beach!

———————

Colin in Helliwell Park, Hornby Island, November

Hornby Island Wish List

I suggest that, in Helliwell Park,
From dawn, until well after dark,
　　They serve chocolate toffee
　　And piping hot coffee
Laced with rum, gin, or fine Cutty Sark!

Like a scene from Arabian Nights
The Thatch would have music and lights
　　And sweet tambourines,
　　While, instead of their jeans,
The girls would go topless, in tights!

———————

✳❤✳

I saw a Venetian wind,
With his clever Venetian mind,
　　Using scissors and strings,
　　Some plastic and things,
A lovely Venetian blind.

───────

A colleague of mine has a car
Bought with pennies he saved in a jar.
　　It has only three wheels,
　　So I know how he feels -
He prefers not to travel too far!

───────

Have you noticed how, down at The Thatch,
Some people just sit there and scratch,
　　While others, it seems,
　　Have impossible dreams -
Of the Senators winning a match?

───────

A Shrubby who lived in the trees
Had dreadlocks right down to his knees;
　　He had chicken manure
　　In his beard, but I'm sure
He was friendly and trying to please!

───────

A herring I'll call Little Mo
Was ever so keen to make roe,
　　But she wasn't to know
　　As she went with the flow
She'll be sushi in downtown To-kyo!

The Mathematical Plumber

In his youth, Richard Morritt, the plumber,
In maths, was a real up-and-comer;
    Even now, as he plumbs,
    He does quick mental sums,
So, in winter, he's still a hot summer!

In his job, he gets cuts and abrasions,
But he's one of those friendly Caucasians,
    He just doesn't care,
    He's learned how to swear
In long, differential equations!

If you find him spaced out while you're talking,
Or when he is sealing or caulking,
    He may be computing
    On a fantasy footing -
A singular feat, while he's walking!

While watching a water-tank draining,
You never hear Richard complaining;
    He's no comedian,
    For things Archimedian
Were part of his graduate training.

Some folk say his looks are quite striking;
He's a fellow you just can't help liking,
    Even when he's engrossed
    In computing the cost
Of an intricate tangle of piping.

_____

An inveterate trav'ler called Rip
Was trashed by a train, on a trip.
    He was dismembered,
    But he'll be remembered -
His tombstone reads - "R.I.P. Rip"!

_____

✳❤✳

A prudish young lady from Lustleigh
Told a young fellow   "You must be
　　Joking if you
　　Think I'm going to screw
And what's more, I insist, leave my bust be!"

──────────

Said a Mafia gangster, all brawn,
"I've a terrible sneeze coming on!
　　I may be a mobster,
　　But I think I've a lobster
Up my nostril - or maybe a prawn!"

──────────

A word that would sure make a nanny grouse -
An adjective - is pusillanimous;
　　They'd apply it to you
　　If you went to the zoo
And were scared by a tiny wee granny mouse.

──────────

When you wake in the dead of the night,
There's nothing compares to the fright,
　　Not even Hell's fires,
　　But your passport expires
Just a day or two prior to your flight!

──────────

I simply can not acquiesce,
If you call this book "vanity press" -
　　It's not so much vanity -
　　But more like insanity -
An uneconomical mess!

✳❤✳

The Lady from Bruges

A very fat lady from Bruges
Decided to take up the luge
    To her deepest chagrin,
    She couldn't get in,
She wasn't just large, she was huge!

Her hair was all higgledy-piggledy,
Her bosom all curvy and jiggley;
    She gave me a smile
    In her sexiest style
And my heart gave a hop, skip and squiggley!

———————

A maiden I knew, on the quiet,
Was oftentimes trying to diet;
    It grew harder each day
    To keep me at bay,
With both of us longing to try it!

———————

A phone freak, Napoleon Bonaparte
Blamed his faults on his folks who had grown apart
    If you rattled his cage
    He'd chew phone books in rage,
Or sometimes he'd just rip his phone apart.

———————

A foxglove we'll call *Digitalis*
Eavesdropping by Buckingham Palace
    Once heard the Dook
    Admonish the cook
Saying "Don't be an old fidget, Alice".

———————

✳❤✳

Another Wedding

When Audrey was still very small,
She was warned about fellows like Paul.
　'Neath a bush in the park
　She was heard to remark
"This don't feel like sinning at all!"

So Audrey's come back after all
And married this chappie named Paul.
　After some months in Ottawa
　The loneliness got to her
- Celibacy started to pall!

From a tiny wee wisp of a thing,
Audrey's big now and wearing a ring
　And Paul can't remember
　A warmer December
With the mattress beginning to spring.

———————

A Canadian with pains in his balls,
To stop falling would cling to the walls,
　He expressed his vexation,
　And pent-up frustration -
"I'm suffering from Viagra falls!"

———————

A shy and retiring factotum
With a simply magnificent scrotum,
　Would agree that its size
　Was a source of surprise,
But he didn't like people to quote 'im.

———————

❤

Said one goddess up there in the sky
"I'm syslexic, dex-mad!", with a sigh,
  "I just never stop -
  Keep those dogs on the hop
And I never let sleeping gods lie"!

———————

Lost Cause in Iraq

As they search 'neath the wide desert sky,
Perhaps you can please tell me why
  Those inspectors are men,
  When they can't find a pen,
Or a sock, or a shirt, or a tie?

But if girls got the job of inspection,
We'd get a much-needed injection
  Of sound common sense,
  Though they can't jump a fence
And haven't much sense of direction.

Seeking weapons of massive destruction
And missile sites under construction,
  Using females *and* males
  Then the whole process fails
- There's a major distraction - seduction!

———————

In Hawaii, you may meet after dark
An ornithophilical shark
  Seeking perfection,
  To augment his collection,
Who'll lop off your leg for a lark!

———————

So Herons are Promiscuous?

A deeply insulted old heron
Didn't like what some folks were inferrin',
    That his morals were loose
    As some raunchy old goose
So, explained one good reason for errin'.

"In spring, it ain't all that surprisin'
That I find a new mate tantalisin';
    I eat, 'til aglow,
    Aphrodisiac roe
And immediately feel the sap risin'!"

He then became rather emphatic
As he talked of his diet, aquatic,
    When a female flew by,
    The raw glint in his eye
Revealed he was getting ecstatic.

I saw we were birds of a feather
Who simply love getting together,
    Not just in spring
    When the sea lions sing,
But all year - and in all kinds of weather!

A councillor over in town
Dived in the Fraser and drowned.
    No one divined
    What he'd dived in to find
Just a penny - or maybe a pound?

✳❤✳

A climber from Western Australia
Tried to conquer a very large dahlia.
While testing his mettle
He fell from a petal,
So the climb was a bit of a fahlia.

———————

High and wet on Shingle Spit   R. Cain

Global Warming Hits Hornby Island

High waves are eroding The Spit,
Global warming is taking the hit
And the sea, day by day,
Eats the shoreline away,
But nobody here gives a shit!

———————

✳❤✳ 149 ✳❤✳

Golfers get January blues
Contending with mud in their shoes,
    Two feet of snow,
    Or 15 below
- And then there's their annual dues!

———————

"Though I *may* seem a trifle aloof,
Like a rook on the ridge of a roof,"
    Said a bull to a cow,
    With an elegant bow
"I'm a bundle of love - on the hoof!"

———————

Out of Proportion

Movie sex doesn't warrant a ripple,
Doesn't cause us to choke on our tipple,
    But you'd think Janet Jackson
    Had sounded a klaxon
When she gave us a glimpse of her nipple!

If you blinked then you'd missed it, I'd say,
Flash of breast with her hand in the way,
    But that demi-second
    When Sinfulness beckoned
Was captured on Instant Replay!

———————

✳❤✳

Limitations and Constraints

A critic of mine, Carol Martin,
Famously known as self-startin',
    Writes speeches with flair,
    (They're not just hot air!)
But finds lim'ricks are harder than fartin'.

As I fought with this rhyme in the night,
I struggled to keep my facts right
    For I knew from the start
    That ladies don't fart
But gentlemen aren't that polite!

—————

Bill Boyd from an emerald asteroid,
A dot in the blue endless vaster void,
    In all that he tried
    Was a failure and died
On his tombstone they called him Disaster Boyd.

—————

Bring on the Dancing Girls!

My right shoulder hurts from a stunt;
My left hip still aches from a dunt.
    My backside is sore,
    I get headaches galore,
But there's nothing much wrong with my front!

—————

✳❤✳

CRITICAL POLITICAL LIMERICKS

Preston Manning has spruced up his image,
Scrapped his specs that he bought in a dim age.
  Contact lenses, he finds,
  Absorb bumps and grinds
In a parliamentarian scrimmage.

Chrétien is no orator - no!
His speeches are muddled and slow!
  When asked to explain,
  He'll always complain,
Shrug his shoulders and say "I don' know"!

The Great Debate - November 2000

I heard all the national debate,
Entertaining, but, sad to relate,
  Jean Chrétien looked tired
  Joe Clark looked re-tyred
But Stockwell had drive and was great!

Alexa had Chrétien on toast,
With his bluster, his bombast and boast;
  Gilles Duceppe had his say
  In a quiet, balanced way,
But Stockwell impressed me the most!

✳❤✳

Stephen Harper seems quite unafraid,
With political savvy displayed,
He's quick on his feet,
Answers questions a treat
- And I like how his jackets are made!

————————

Who'll run the Conservative flock?
Belinda brings more than just talk,
But one niggling question
Gives me indigestion
- Is she running before she can walk?

————————

Clement has a crowning fixation,
He wants to do good for the nation.
Nice-looking and bright,
I imagine he might
Be welcome at most nurses' stations.

————————

Fiscal prudence, Paul Martin declares,
But - more millions for Indian Affairs,
For the lawyers and chiefs
With their leftist beliefs -
The poor taxpayer simply despairs.

————————

And now there's the Sponsorship Scandal
A credit to Hun, Goth or Vandal
A cool hundred million
Went zippety-zillion
For Martin it's too hot to handle!

✳❤✳

"We'll get to the bottom of this!"
Is the mantra the Liberals hiss,
    When asked to explain
    Their gravy-boat train
And the millions continually missed.

————————

Anger - it surely gets mine up -
All handguns and long guns must sign up.
    Two billion for this?
    It's bureaucrats' bliss
And there aren't any crooks in the lineup!

————————

At tax time my feelings are tender
When I see all the cash I surrender
    And it's frittered away!
    Politicians play
With our dollars like drunks on a bender!

————————

Via Rail and the RCMP
Were in on the Sponsorship spree;
    They claim they're like roses,
    We're holding our noses,
It smells like corruption to me!

————————

Passports all neatly embossed,
It seems thirty thousand are lost!
    A security list
    simply doesn't exist,
So the bad guys keep coming across!

✳❤✳

THINK ABOUT IT!

See You later - Hallucinator!

God may see each sparrow fall,
Each lily lazing in the field,
But won't deflect the lightning ball
Or cause my enemies to yield.

Some instant from The Great Explosion,
Did God lose interest in His plan
Which, worn from aeons of erosion,
Contained the Rise and Fall of Man?

Hallucinations, grief-related,
Explain the Resurrection myth,
While Paul, apostle, contemplated,
Then wrote the Christian creed forthwith.

Grin and bear it in this strifetime,
Future, everlasting joy,
But beyond the present lifetime
 - Eternal Life - a salesman's ploy?

To view delights with circumspection -
The brandished stick, the fires of Hell,
But avoid the thorny question
 - Eternal Death - a harder sell?

As one religion fades away,
Another blooms and takes its place;
Beyond the farthest stars' array
God smiles, amazement on His face.

✳❤✳

This next poem is translated from the Swedish and is printed here with the permission of the copyright-holder of the original verses. It was written by Nils Johan Einar Ferlin (1898-1961) and was entitled "Inte Ens":

Not Even

Not even a grey, tiny birdie
That sings on a greening bough,
Will you find on that other shoreline
- How drab it all seems to me now.

Not even a grey, tiny birdie
And never a birch that stands white,
But on the loveliest day that the summer can give
I have sometimes longed for that sight.

✳❤✳

A Coin In The Water

I gaze from the pier at the mirrored reflection
Of fishboats, their masts and their spidery shrouds,
Their colourful floats - and on further inspection,
I see they are sailing on silvery clouds.

And here there's a patch of mercurial brightness,
A break in the grey of the dull leaden sky,
Close to the rip-rap that borders the sea-shore,
A brightness that captures the wandering eye.

Firstly I see just the glistening surface
Enriched with an elegant, pewtery glow,
Marred for a moment, a shimmering ripple -
A tiny fish darts in the waters below.

My eyes focus farther, on clouds 'neath the surface,
Bright lines where adjacent soft billowings join,
They steadily drift, and then, to my amazement,
The sun is revealed as a bright silver coin.

I pensively wonder, perhaps it may be
A coin for the boatman who's waiting for me?

✳❤✳

Global Warning - Apocalypse Soon?

Just how rosy is the Future's
Apocalyptic rosy glow?
Short-sightedly we shun the suture
That might the dreaded nine forego.

Greenhouse gases boil and burgeon,
Fossil fuels get all the blame;
Pollution kills the ancient sturgeon
Who knows not whence pollution came.

Never fear, the crunch approaches,
(Don't buy that big and bright machine!)
Amidst our moans and loud reproaches
Comes a hike in gasoline.

Some dream, pure green, of wind and solar,
Think all technology amiss -
The problem's scope is circumpolar,
Their rhetoric is wind and piss!

All the Third World's teeming millions'
Wants and needs are ever higher -
Burning kilowatts in trillions,
To be like us, their dreams aspire.

China's path we should proclaim
With its strict one-family-child;
If India could but do the same
To stop its numbers running wild!

We run like some beheaded pullet
In circles round a smoking pyre,
So we must bite the bitter bullet,
Seek some secret unknown fire.

＊♥＊

The quest demands such untold treasure
The First World only can provide;
The Third World's help in other measure
Could stem its population tide.

The prize is great, can market forces,
Despite the politicians' pout,
Summon the required resources
Before the sands of Time run out?

Before the Maldives' disappearing,
And Bangladeshis slowly drown',
We need some brilliant engineering
Before the Ship of Earth goes down.

Mobile Phone Plague

I see all these people with phones to their ear,
In a bus, on the street, in a tram
And wonder, if ever we all disappear,
Will the stars in the sky give a damn?

❤

Parting, In a Dream

She left.
I felt my body separate,
Limb from limb
And flesh from bone;
A thread, bright red,
Pursued the knife
On flesh as cold as stone.

Did our parents feel the same
When we left our hearth - for fame?

Baileguish Croft, Kincraig, Inverness-shire

A rusty bedstead blocks the door
So no one passes.
Tumbled stones vie on the floor
With weeds and grasses.

No roof to hide the stony gable,
Stark and lonely.
The laughter round the kitchen table
- A memory only.

The grass is green and smooth, outside,
Still strangely neat.
No barefoot children run and hide
Round stacks of peat.

Scattered wide and wandered far
From hearth and home,
On foreign strand, 'neath frozen star,
The children roam.

✳❤✳

HEADING FOR THE FINISH LINE

Not Enough Time

This poem's a poem for everyone who
I've met and enjoyed through the years,
For the guys and the dolls and acquaintances too,
Who've shared all my laughter and tears;
For the fellows I've argued with, girls that I've kissed
Or maybe just slapped on the bum,
Shared a walk through a park in the gathering mist
Or a juicy Victoria plum.

Boilers and badminton, tennis and tea,
A conference, meeting or chore,
A dip in a lake or a swim in the sea
Or a walk on a desolate shore.

Perhaps I have written a poem before
- A rhyme just especially for you -
If I haven't, I should have, but ran out of time
Though I lived to a hundred and two.

The Lure of Heaven?

Edward Lear and Thomas Hood
(Death did not divide them!)
I revere and if I'm good,
I'll get to sit beside them!

Hangin' in there!

In the days of my youth, boy - did I get a thrill
As long as the maid wasn't fashioned of ice!
Though I may be older, the girls look the same
- The buzz from my hearing aid doesn't suffice!

What a Bargain!

They've just replaced my Tilley hat,
'Twas guaranteed for life!
Sixteen summers, fancy that -
I strut before my wife!

The face beneath the brim is older,
Somewhat lined, it's true,
But the hat is jaunty, bolder,
Dashing, spanking new!

My brand new hat allays my hunger
For vanished youth (boo hoo!) -
Our average age is eight years younger
And I feel younger too!

Inexorable - Tough!

Age keeps creeping, while we're sleeping,
While we're waking, overtaking
All our sweetly youthful fears.

Skin a-wrinkling, Hell's bells tinkling,
That's the ringing in your ears!

Make the Most of It

I smell a rose and just a whiff
Sets me up for hours, as if
My blood were rampant, pounding, red,
And all directions lead - to bed!

So let's enjoy these golden years,
Ignore dark Death and all his fears,
Grinning skull-like o'er my shoulder -
That sort of thought just makes you older!

Dead, a long time, we will be
So let's enjoy life merrily -
Enjoy our friends, their fun and laughter
And we'll live happy ever after!

Twinkle, Twinkle!

Sixty! All downhill from here
Is the litany I hear!
I don't believe a word for I
Still have a twinkle in my eye!

No Dinosaur

Just like a coelacanth under the sea,
To Youth, I'm a dinosaur, old as can be.
In truth, I have hundreds of fishes to fry
And I still have a gleam in my coelacanth eye!

＊❤＊

Sore Toe

It feels like I've arthritis in my foot,
I visualize it, twisted, like a root,
    Bent and all knobbly,
    Walking all wobbly,
    Schachlin' and hobbly,
    Grouchy old Man!

I doubt that it's gout,
For that's an affliction
Shared by princes and kings,
Emperors, potentates, other such things,
Caused by excess of urea (whose ear?),
A highly unlikely prediction.

The doctor says the problem is my arch
And it's *not* triumphal when I march,
    Longing once more to be
    Fit as a flying flea
    'Cause I don't want to be
    Grouchy old man!

I like to dispel the illusion
That I'm quickly becoming a wreck,
Though it will but increase the confusion
    When I say that the pain
    In my foot is no sprain,
    But simply a pain in the neck!

And as I suffer the hirpling and hobbling
Pains that are catching my breath,
    I look on the bright side,
    For back in the days
    Of hunting and gathering,
    Walking and wandering,
    Not to walk was - Death!

✳❤✳

Post-Wine-Club-Meeting Trauma .. Or.....

I woke, my heart was beating strangely,
Remembering a crescent moon.
Pulse unsteady, took an aspirin,
Hope this passes rather soon!

What would make my heart beat wildly
Like a roller-coaster ride?
Was it wine - or Death's Bright Angel's
Signal from the other side?

Hours and hours until the dawning;
Time, uncaring, like a stone;
Should I waken Jane, or tremble
In the darkness, all alone?

Grab a pen and piece of paper,
This small verse may be my last!
A pity, there's so much to conquer
- I'd like to have a longer past!

PS: Made it!

See you later - Fibrillator

It seems that my heart's palpitation
Is atrial-type fibrillation
    And the thought, not so hot,
    Is - a clot from that spot
May render me *ex* circulation.

✳❤✳

Get Focussed!!!

The fact is, life's slipping away,
Though you thought it had come here to stay!
    Cut down on employment!
    Get much more enjoyment!
Take time off from working - and PLAY!!!

The summer's get shorter, it seems
And less realistic, our dreams!
    You have to remember,
    That, now it's November
It never just rains - it just teems!

Give your sweetie a kiss and rub noses!
Take a stroll where the primrose reposes!
    If you don't, then you'll find
    Regrets filling your mind
When the time comes to push up the roses!

If you climb out of bed with a sigh
And you don't feel especially spry,
    Life has lots more to give,
    Get focussed and LIVE!
Raise your glasses - here's mud in your eye!!!

✳❤✳

Waste Not, Want Not!

Just one bite upon the cherry,
Life is but a single rose;
Don't waste one chance of making merry,
Nor a second, being morose!

In Youth, we tread the straight and narrow,
Life has no apparent end;
Now one fears Life's speeding arrow
May end up going round the bend!

Before, we ran each mile in minutes,
Testosterone decided much;
Now Wisdom recognizes limits
But doesn't yet require a crutch!

As down the pathway, now you teeter
Towards the light that beckons there,
Savour moments, ever sweeter,
Caress your lover's silv'ring hair!

✳❤✳

'Twas Simply a Cough That Carried Me Off!

I had a dreadful bout of coughing
Which lasted more than half an hour!
I thought that Death was in the offing,
Haemorrhage, his brightest flower!

It seems I've got a virus.
(Doesn't coughing tire us?
I'd love to get some sleep!)

Life has such fragility;
I try to think Tranquillity:
Rivers running deep,

Patterns on the ocean floor,
Ripples on a distant shore,
Stars that stretch for evermore,
A ruined, ancient keep.

I guess I've got the bug of rhyming,
Really inconvenient timing;
Will anybody weep?

Four Seasons

Spring 's a lovely memory,
Summer was a song,
Hurtling through an autumn sunset,
Maybe Winter won't be long?

Colin, on the right side of the tombstone,
in Coldingham Priory Churchyard, Berwickshire, Scotland

Birthday Greetings

In another ten years time,
I may be a ghost, sublime,
Travelling at the speed of light
On a moonbeam through the night,
Irrespective of the weather!
    Going Wooo-ooo-ooo-ooo!

And the reason I'm not blue
Is - you may be a spirit too
And we'll haunt the world together!

We'll visit all our Absent Friends
In a jaunt that never ends!
    Going Wooo-ooo-ooo-ooo!

INDEX OF FIRST LINES

✳❤✳

✳❤✳